YOU DON'T HAVE TO LIVE ALONE

How Seniors Can Find Companionship or Marriage

by

Carl Metzger, M.D.

MAGNI

Copyright © 2011 The Magni Group, Inc.

email: info@magnico.com

Website: www.magnico.com

ISBN: 978-1-882330-87-4

About the Author

As a physician, media consultant and writer, Dr.Metzger has been dedicated to the power of human relationships for over 40 years. After receiving his M.D. degree in 1968 he went on to train in child and family psychiatry. Then, as a Major in the Air Force, he helped support the emotional health of families of overseas military members for three years. His subsequent office practice consisted of facilitating relationships in families, marriages and individuals. He hosted "Healthline", a radio talk show devoted to social and community issues that listeners brought to his attention. He was called upon often by TV anchors, other radio hosts and newspapers to give opinion or advice. (In the aftermath of the Oklahoma City bombings he helped to mediate a national radio call-in). On many occasions he spoke at schools, seminars and community groups. He has written, and is in the process of writing, several other books in addition to YOU DON'T HAVE TO LIVE ALONE, including THE SECRET TO HAPPY CHILDREN AND GRANDCHILDREN. He presently offers discussions and expertise through his website drcarlmetzger.com., conducts seminars, and generally enjoys living in New York City with his wife and two dogs.

TABLE OF CONTENTS

INTRODUCTION

I know a lot about your present situation. I know how much you want to be cared for, and how much you want to be in a relationship with a very nice person. I know it is always somewhat on your mind. You may think about it a little, or a lot, depending on who you are with, what you are doing and how circumstances are affecting you.

You've been trying to find this special person for what seems like a long time. You have tried to remain optimistic and not to feel desperate. You feel like you're always scanning the people around you, judging and evaluating.

Those who don't measure up to what you're looking for seem very numerous. Those that do measure up seem out of reach or already taken. The more time goes by the more likely you are to feel old or unattractive.

If you were in a good relationship earlier in your life you may feel it can never be duplicated. The relationships that didn't work out seem confusing, and have you asking yourself who was to blame. Asking friends for support has often resulted in advice that you couldn't really use. There was also the fear that those friends were getting a little tired and frustrated with you. There have been times you felt it would be easier to give up the idea of finding someone, but this only caused you to feel sad.

Yes, I know a lot about your situation and I want to maximize your chances of meeting, and keeping, somebody special. And so, I offer you YOU DON'T HAVE TO LIVE ALONE. In this book I will talk to you straight and clear. I will help you make sense of your behavior and feelings. I will support your efforts to find someone and provide understanding and reassurance in the topics presented.

HOW SENIORS CAN FIND COMPANIONSHIP OR MARRIAGE

You see, I have been doing the work of understanding and maximizing relationships for almost forty years.

Trained as a medical doctor, then specializing in the mental health field, I have talked with individuals, couples, and families about the interactions and experiences that make life special and worthwhile. In addition to my office practice, I hosted a radio talk show for over ten years and took part in numerous TV, radio and newspaper interviews and articles. Over and over I have seen how loneliness can be overcome; I have seen new interests and new relationships add a spark to life and a renewed sense of life's pleasures.

On a personal level you should know that I have had a long marriage, with loving children and grandchildren.

Therefore, both professionally and personally I feel well trained and well experienced to offer you this important book.

In YOU DON'T HAVE TO LIVE ALONE, I will talk about the many things that play a part in the search for someone special. Some will make sense to you immediately. Others will sink in more slowly.

I will explore with you the way you dress and the way you eat; I will also go over things you should feel proud of as well as things you don't feel good about. I will help you stop behavior that is not working well for you and suggest behavior that will work better. Even though you can't actually tell me what you are thinking you will get a sense that I already have some idea about it.

As you read over the Table of Contents, you will find no obvious rationale for how the topics are presented.

This random listing is done for a reason. All the topics are important and you are encouraged to read them as you are curious and as they appeal to you.

At the end of YOU DON'T HAVE TO LIVE ALONE you will find a wonderful Opportunity and Resource Section. It will provide ideas and practical information for your search. Look through it at your leisure. As you get an increasing sense of confidence and hope from reading the YOU DON'T HAVE TO LIVE ALONE topics, you will find this section will seem more exciting and valuable to you. There is also a Special Care Section - for living so you never feel alone.

You may want to introduce YOU DON'T HAVE TO LIVE ALONE to friends or family so they, too, will be available for sharing ideas and support.

Thank you for giving me the opportunity to talk with you about your very important search. You deserve a wonderful relationship, and by reading YOU DON'T HAVE TO LIVE ALONE you will most surely find one.

With you all the way to success,

Carl Metzger

YOUR SOCIAL WORLD

The Land of Opportunity

Wherever you meet and mingle with your friends is your social world. It is where you expect to have fun and be stimulated by those who you know or who you can meet. It is an alternative to those other worlds where something is expected of you and where your choices are limited. In those other worlds you spend your time and energy doing tasks, fulfilling routines or taking care of others.

If you work behind a desk at the insurance company, your focus is on providing service to your customers. If you do the laundry every Wednesday, you need your detergent and a working washing machine. If your beagle needs walking, you have to pay attention to other dogs and whether she does her business.

In these "non-social" worlds the chances of meeting a new and interesting person are somewhat limited. It can happen but your attention is elsewhere, your preparation to be social is minimal, and you may not present yourself as attractively as possible.

It is in your social world that meeting somebody special has the best chance of happening. Your chances will be greatest when you create opportunities that work. These opportunities depend on *variety*, *flexibility* and *innovation*.

If you meet your friends every Friday night at the same pizza place, you may get your hunger satisfied and enjoy talking with your friends, but meeting someone new becomes unlikely.

How Seniors Can Find Companionship or Marriage

Maximize your chances to meet someone special Friday evening by:

Variety - Suggest eating at different places, with different kinds of food…. perhaps in different neighborhoods as well.

Flexibility – Suggest going out a different night, sometimes early, sometimes later. Be willing to go out a fewer number of friends if some can't go.

Innovation – Give other eating situations a chance…. perhaps a neighborhood happy hour, or the occasional church supper.

Creating opportunities to meet someone socially is something you have to work at. Keeping a "social activity journal" can be helpful. When you have a written record of places, times, who you were with, and who seemed to be available, it makes you more efficient at planning and using your social time to greatest advantage.

Thinking about meeting someone in this objective way makes it a more effective part of your planning. It makes socializing less emotional and more like dealing with your customers, doing your wash or walking your beagle…. something you do dependably and well.

Your social world can become a land of opportunity, but you must play your part in making the opportunity happen.

FAMILY ISSUES

Meeting all Needs

Since your beginning, family has been where you looked for, and expected your care. It took years of experiencing care in other places for you to expand your care expectations. First it was extended family, then friends, and most likely you've had a significant other in your past.

In your search to find a new partner it will help you to use the positive issues in your family, and not be deterred by the negative issues.

I suspect there are family members that expect you to take care of them in some ways. It may be a daughter who has young children of her own. She depends on you to be there when she needs to talk, to help her with childcare and babysitting. She likes you to be available. It seems like she really needs you.

You may have an elderly father who lives nearby and is on his own. It's getting hard for him to drive, he has doctors' appointments to get to, and he loves when you visit and bring him food.

Your daughter and your father could both be considered negative family issues. They take time and energy. Their needs may interfere with your social time.

You may feel pulled in different directions when you try to make time for your social activities. It's not easy to be in two places at once. After taking care of family, you may not have the energy to go out and socialize.

It's important to understand that these family situations can be turned into positive opportunities for everybody concerned. To do so you must believe the following: You come first – and by putting yourself first everyone will benefit. Here's how it works.

Once you've met your special person you will seem happier, stronger and more involved with the world. Your messages to your family will be more positive and your responses to their needs will take less energy. Seeing how you take care of your partner will reassure your children about your ability to take care of them. Your father won't be losing a companion; he'll be gaining a new source of companionship. Seeing your happiness will make him less likely to feel guilty about the help you provide.

Finding the right relationship is about expanding your world; everyone in your family who lives there will benefit.

CUSTOMS AND CONVENTIONS

Yours are Most Important

When you follow customs and conventions you are supposedly acting "in the right way". Or to say it differently, you are being a good person and doing the right thing.

When you are searching for, and entering into, a new relationship, you want to feel as good as possible about what you are doing, and how you are conducting yourself. The better you feel about yourself, the more attractive you will be to your special person.

However, the definition of custom and convention can become blurred in finding and forming a permanent relationship. What you want to do is often at odds with what you think you should (or should not) do.

For example, you are at a social gathering at your church talking to single friends who are regulars there. Someone you haven't seen before comes over to join the group. In a few minutes, you realize that the two of you are involved in a very pleasant and intense conversation. This continues until a cell phone interrupts and your friends tell you they have to leave immediately. Now you are faced with a choice: Obey custom and convention and let this new person slip away (after all, you hardly know them; also you owe some loyalty to your single friends). Or, take the bold step necessary to further this possible relationship. The bold step is to clearly state that you've enjoyed the conversation, that you would like the opportunity to continue getting to know each other and then offer your name and phone number.

Custom and convention exist to give some order to society and to keep people comfortable. But relationships – especially intimate ones – exist to give deep and forever care. In other words, respect custom and convention – but don't let them rule the day if they threaten your chances of having someone special in your life. Apply this to the process of meeting, getting to know someone and becoming physically involved with them. This all contributes to your personal care which should take priority over custom and convention.

YOUR BODY

Like It and Another Will Also

There are three ways that you maintain a sense of your body – how it feels to you, how it looks in the mirror and how others seem to be responding to it. So which way is most important when it comes to liking your body?

If you have arthritis in your knees climbing steps will be painful. You may get angry and feel that your body is letting you down. If your arms are heavy you may be bothered every time you pull on a shirt. In these situations the way you feel physically may cause you to dislike your body.

Looking in the mirror can be a terrible and repetitive activity. If you think your face doesn't look attractive you can be sure it will be your face that you look at first in the mirror.

If you think you have a big belly, then your belly will get your first look. The reason this happens is that you hope the mirror image will change but you are also sure that it won't. This is a maddening situation and makes looking at you in the mirror an unlikable experience.

With all these negative feelings about your body how can you like it more and, most important, how can you have a companion or spouse who likes it and loves to interact physically with you.

When somebody loves you – your attitude, your ability to give care, your outlook on life – they will love your body as an extension of all your good qualities. But in addition you have to present your body in the right way.

Don't say negative things about it ("I feel so fat", I have so many wrinkles", "I don't have the strength I used to").

Rather, make positive comments about the way you feel about your body ("My skin feels very soft today", "My legs feel like they have a lot of energy") and, equally important, comment positively about the physical contact you are having with your partner ("I get such a nice feeling when you hold my hand", "When you hug me I feel so secure").

This way of presenting your body will make it feel likeable and attractive – to your significant other, and to you.

INFIRMITY

Turn it to Your Advantage

When you are looking for a relationship, one of the questions in your mind may be "Who would want me?" This is a natural question since being close to someone not only has to do with what you want from them, but also what they want from you.

What you are basically considering is your worth. The more you are worth, the more someone will want you. To really be wanted is the goal of great romance. It promises great care and a feeling of special worth.

So it is very important to feel you are worth someone's attention and love. This may be difficult if you have a medical or physical issue – some infirmity.

Infirmity implies weakness – if a recent surgery makes normal movement difficult, if a medical condition requires dietary monitoring, if medication is required during the day or if regular doctors' appointments are part of your routine – these all can make you feel vulnerable or weak. Feeling this way makes it hard to think you have enough worth to attract someone significant.

You may be stuck with your "infirmities" but you can manage them in ways that preserve your strength and independence. In so doing you will save your own feelings of worth and appear attractive to another.

First, make your "infirmity routine" seem under your control rather than controlling you. For example, if you are telling your companion about a doctor's appointment, you can say something like, "I'm going to make my doctor's day and pay him a visit".

How Seniors Can Find Companionship or Marriage

Second, make something that may seem burdensome appear to be "fun". For example, when it comes time to taking all your pills, you can say something like, "I can't wait to take that pile of candy".

Third, if some aspect of your physical condition becomes obvious when you're with your partner, make it something to be shared and overcome together. For example, if you develop shortness of breath going up an incline, you can say something like, "Give me your arm and we'll beat this hill together".

Using "infirmity" as a way of increasing your attractiveness will "firm up" your romantic life.

STAYING FIT

Is it Really Necessary

What exactly is "fit"? It doesn't say what your heart rate should be, how fast you should swim a lap, or how many jumping jacks you can do. It doesn't even say what you should weigh.

"Fit" is a general and descriptive term that has to do with how you rate yourself physically and how you are rated by others.

The most important way to evaluate your "fitness" is by how much your physical activities contribute to your personal enjoyment of life. You also want to avoid the common idea that a high level of fitness helps to attract a partner.

How often have you heard friends say "I want to lose the pounds so I'll get noticed" or, "Maybe my sex life will improve if I firm up these thighs"?

In fact, being "noticed" is mostly a function of what kind of positive signals you give out clearly and consistently. For example, your sex life will improve best by giving your partner tender care while expressing pleasure during sex. As you can see, in this situation fitness is not the major factor.

The role of fitness in a relationship is both personal and mutual. On a personal basis it allows you to feel both comfortable and strong. A good workout can produce a sense of calm well-being as well as a sense of energy and optimism. These kinds of feelings are bound to attract, and keep, a partner.

HOW SENIORS CAN FIND COMPANIONSHIP OR MARRIAGE

Mutual fitness discussions with your partner about what would feel good (a nice walk after dinner, a bike ride on the weekend) and what would be healthy (changes in diet, a gym membership) can make your relationship more interesting and fun.

To sum up the connection between fitness and forming a relationship: You don't have to be "fit" to develop a relationship, but a relationship can be improved by both of you staying fit together.

FANTASIES ABOUT CLOSENESS

Sweet Thinking

Fantasies are like dark chocolate – they can be delicious but also bittersweet. As with chocolate you turn to fantasies as a way of getting pleasure. When they involve a member of the opposite sex, their purpose is to provide a relationship (in your head only) that is completely under your control. In your fantasy the other person knows what you need and provides closeness in some way.

It feels best if you are fantasizing about being close to someone you already know or are involved with. This means that your fantasy is based on some knowledge or experience of this person. There is enough reality present to make the closeness seem possible and likely to increase over time. This closeness fantasy is easy to have and leaves you feeling sweet and hopeful when it is over.

However, if you are fantasizing about someone you may have only seen briefly or from a distance, or have made up completely, you may not get the desired result. You may find yourself feeling sad or hopeless after the fantasy is over. This is because the better your fantasy partner gives you closeness the more you may be thinking that it is unlikely that you will ever meet anyone like this. This can become a bittersweet experience that doesn't do what you want it to.

suggest that you do the following to make your closeness fantasies not only feel good but actually help you find a significant relationship:

1 – Keep a journal of the types of fantasies you are having. The three types of closeness fantasies are: *physical closeness involving sexual activities*, *physical closeness involving touch* (hugging, holding

How Seniors Can Find Companionship or Marriage

hands, and being near each other), and *closeness that is not yet complete* (going toward each other, watching each other, the fantasy person talking about you or knowing about you).

2 – Decide which type feels best.

3 – Write the names of those potential partners that you already know, or that you meet, that best fit your fantasy.

4 – Fantasize and use as a guide to potential partners.

This process will help you use your closeness fantasies constructively and get the most pleasure from them – without the bittersweet aftertaste.

LIFE EXPERIENCE

Helps You Pick the Best

In your search to find a significant partner you need every advantage possible. The bigger the advantage, the greater your chance for success. Your life experience represents such an advantage. What you need to do is separate the positive things you've learned about people from the negative things you may have experienced with them.

A good partner is like a ripe tomato. Before you pluck it you have to find it, inspect it and give it a squeeze. You don't want to choose a rotten tomato. Through your adult years you have come in contact with people who made you laugh, helped you feel secure and seemed to value your company. Those are qualities that represent what you desire in a relationship. Your life experience should teach you that this kind of person has to be sought out.

But you shouldn't stop looking because you haven't found one for yourself yet. Your experience tells you that ripe tomatoes exist and you keep looking in the tomato patch until you find one.

When you think you've met someone with the right qualities, you spend time getting to know them because your experience has made you careful about first impressions. But you don't decide early on that they are too good to be true. When you come upon a bright red tomato on the vine you bring it close and inspect its entire surface before being confident enough to pick it.

Believing you may have met the right person your life experience advises a trial of intimacy and some dependence to really make a wise decision. But you don't tumble head over heels toward commitment.

HOW SENIORS CAN FIND COMPANIONSHIP OR MARRIAGE

Holding what appears to be a perfectly colored and shaped tomato you give it your expert squeezes to really be sure it is ready to pass your lips.

Lover or farmer, it is your life experience positively applied that helps you make the best choice.

YOUR PARTNER'S AGE

It May not Matter

Looking for a companion or marriage partner is a search for qualities – qualities of care-giving that will make you feel special, secure and attractive. It makes sense that you look for these qualities within the groups that you are most familiar with. These groups are the people you live with, work with, or socialize with. Chances are that most are about your age. Is this a good thing for your search or not?

Certainly when you are looking to meet someone special it helps to be in reassuring circumstances. People of your age can provide that. It's nice to know that the person you are interested in has "been there, done that". It starts you out on the same page, and there is a sense that you are familiar with the same things.

You may have similar issues with your adult children, or share experiences regarding divorce, the death of a spouse, or the loneliness of doing things by yourself.

This all seems to make a strong case for a partner of the same age. In fact, most people finding a new relationship pick someone within the same age group. It seems to be the easier way and I think there are real advantages of this choice – advantages of reassuring circumstances and mutually familiar experiences.

However, in searching for someone outside your age group, you may find excitement or wisdom that can be very wonderful. Sharing physical activities with someone younger – from biking to sex – can offer new life possibilities and a sense of renewal. Engaging in conversation and social activities with someone older can offer a rewarding chance to provide care while learning about life in a new way.

How Seniors Can Find Companionship or Marriage

Which way to go? In your search for a significant person, are you best off choosing people that are older, younger, or the same age? The best strategy is to focus on the goals and qualities that you know are important to you. This is far more important than the age of the person. If someone is older in age but optimistic and vital in their living, choose them. If someone is younger in age but seems settled and satisfied, choose them.

Engage socially in your usual age group and in different age groups. This will give you the broadest choices and the best chances.

ACTING STRONG

The Quality that Attracts

If you asked me which is the most attractive quality someone can have – I would say "strength", without a doubt. It is the quality that can bring you the best and the most that life can offer. It is the quality that will attract someone special to you like a bee is attracted to honey.

Strength is the long term quality that provides hope when life gets difficult, that helps one live a life of goodness, and that keeps two people faithful. Being such an important quality, your display of strength will be noticed by the person you are interested in, and will be very attractive to them.

When a relationship is forming there are several basic phases where your display of strength is most important.

These phases are: *First Contact*, *Ongoing Contact*, and *Expanding Contact*. It will be helpful to give you some examples of acting strong (with your words) in each of these three phases.

> *First Contact* – When you realize there is someone you would like to meet – here are some strong ways to proceed: If the person of interest is not physically there with you say to someone who knows them, "Ask them for their phone number and tell them I'll be calling" or, "Give them my phone number and say I'd like them to call me" or, if the person of interest is physically present say to someone who knows them "Take me over and introduce me" or, directly to the person of interest, "I think it would be good for both of us to get to know each other".

Ongoing Contact – When you've started speaking to someone of interest or are beginning to see them regularly, be clear about how the relationship is progressing.

Strong comments are: "It was very good that we met", or, "It seems we share a lot in common", or, "I know we're going to enjoy getting to know each other".

Expanding Contact – As you both realize your relationship is becoming important and as future plans come into your discussions, these are some strong statements to keep things moving forward: "We are learning a lot about each other and I'm sure there will be a lot more to learn", or, "Together we seem to get a lot out of life", or, "Our relationship is just as good as I hoped it would be".

What all of these suggested comments have in common is that you sound strong, that you know what is good for both of you, and that you are able to put that into effective words.

Any person with this kind of strength is one worth getting to know and hanging onto. You can be that person.

You Don't Have to Live Alone

THE SUBJECT OF MONEY

Buying Happiness

You don't need me to tell you that money can be difficult as well as wonderful. What you might need me to tell you is how to manage the subject of money as you look to get into a meaningful relationship.

As money provides all kinds of care (food, personal services, shoes, etc.), people tend to be attracted to it, and to whoever seems to have it. If you have lots of money you might question the motives of someone new getting close to you. If you have little money you might question your own motives in getting close to someone who is financially well off.

As you are looking for, or getting into, a new relationship, the best way to handle the subject of money is as minimally and neutrally as possible.

This means not connecting money to how you feel ("It makes me scared to think about not having enough money when I retire"), not appearing to have money affecting the quality of your life ("I feel guilty spending any money on myself"), and not inquiring about the other person's assets ("Do you have a lot of money in stocks?").

To avoid money coming between you and a new romantic partner, be straight and minimal in your discussions about it. Say what is necessary and what the situation calls for. This includes what things cost, paying for things when you are together, or discussing money topics that may arise socially or in the media. If you find yourself getting anxious or angry about a discussion of money, be prepared to say something like, "It's interesting how money can stir things up between people. I think that's happening with us".

_____ **37** _____

This can serve as a way to change the current discussion while introducing some caution for the future.

Of course money discussions evolve and become more candid over time but that assumes that a trusting and mutually dependent relationship has been established.

Remember, money can buy happiness, but only when you and your partner handle it wisely and respectfully.

RUNNING OUT OF TIME

Wanting Someone Now

What could be worse that knowing what you want but being afraid you will never get it? When something is very important to you – like a meaningful relationship – not having it now easily leads to the thought of never having it. Time becomes a negative factor and the more you think about it, the more your search for someone special seems under pressure.

You probably know that you are more aware of time when you are uncomfortable in some way. When you are happy and things are going well, you may not think about the passing of time at all.

When you are in the process of finding a partner, the issue of time is often front and center – "How can I make the time to meet someone?" (Socialization takes time), "How quickly can I learn to trust someone?" (You know it's got to take time), "How long will it take to really get to know someone?" (Experiences and personality factors take time to process).

You may hear your friends speak about this idea of time running out, but for them it may serve a negative purpose – to receive sympathy or attention. Try not to become part of that conversation because saying and agreeing that time is running out makes it seem more of a fact.

What you should be telling yourself is that there is plenty of time to find someone – this will help you be more energetic, hopeful, and smart in your search and will make you exactly the kind of person who is successful in getting into a relationship – quickly.

How Seniors Can Find Companionship or Marriage

SMART DRESSING

Be Attractive Comfortably

Although it's true that you can't always tell a book by its cover, any experienced bookseller will tell you it's the cover that makes the reader pick the book up.

You want to be the book that is picked up, examined, and taken home with the excited reader. Your cover is the way you dress – the clothes you choose, how you wear them and which of your features they emphasize. Your smart choice of clothes can make it much easier to attract and keep a future companion or spouse.

When you are out socially, you certainly want to dress in an attractive way, but you don't want to do it at the expense of your basic comfort. It would not be smart to wear heels that are too high, a skirt that is too short or a blouse that shows too much cleavage.

Although that type of dressing may attract initial attention, your level of increased awkwardness and self-consciousness could drive the attention away.

It's logical to think that to meet new people you must have a new style of dressing (a "new you"). What you don't want to do is adopt a style that is radically different from how you usually dress. It is better to keep your usual style – and perhaps update and intensify it. Good examples include how you wear shoes and sweaters.

With shoes, if you like to walk around in sandals, find new sandals that have a low heel. If your standard color has been brown, find a pair that is bright red. You'll still retain the comfort of wearing familiar type shoes but you'll also know your

HOW SENIORS CAN FIND COMPANIONSHIP OR MARRIAGE

new shoes will make you look more feminine and sexy (red is the ultimate signal that you are interested).

Considering sweaters, your choice can make you either a nice but uninteresting person or an intriguing and desirable candidate for closeness. Stick to my advice – retain your comfort while at the same time adding pizzazz to your image. If your sweaters have been primarily for the purpose of covering your upper body and if your color choice ranges from grey to various pastels – try the following: wear sweaters that have buttons – then leave the top few unbuttoned. This adds a bit of tease and also allows for your neck to be more exposed – so someone special can fantasize about snuggling into it. To make yourself even more noticeable choose a bright color – this will be visually attracting as your underlying upper body will be more in focus.

Smart dressing really means being smart about how you dress. You want to feel like your usual self while dressing attractively in new and unusual ways.

BEING SEXUAL

Excitement in a Nice Way

The word "sex" is much too short and simple for what can be both a pleasurable as well as a problem behavior. As you are thinking about a new relationship, and as sexual behavior will certainly be part of that, you want to get the most pleasure and the least problems from that activity.

When you are meeting a new person of interest you wonder about the kind of sexual behavior that will take place. Your thoughts (and the other person's) will have to do with such things as attractiveness, sexual preferences and experience, and making sex a regular part of your lives together.

The best way to proceed with sexual behavior is slowly. Even though you and your new companion have a history of sexuality (you both have probably been sexually active in the past, but at different frequencies, with a single or multiple partners, and with more or less satisfaction) you should put off sex while other important things take place.

First, you should be establishing a sense of mutual attractiveness – both in terms of physical appearance as well as a desire to be with each other. Second, there should be a sense of moving into the future together. When these are in process you have set up a security base that helps sexual behavior to develop in the best way. If your partner seems to become impatient , say clearly and strongly that you are looking forward to great sex and taking it slow is the best way to make that happen.

Once you have become sexual together there are General Guidelines and Mind and Body Advice to insure that your pleasure is great and problems are minimal:

General Guidelines:

- Don't feel guilty if you shy away from certain sexual behaviors. You can discuss what it is that your partner likes about that type of sex and assure them that you will keep it under consideration. The discussions will give you both ideas and insight about your preferences. Discussing things this way makes them less emotional and encourages mutual respect.

- Don't make comparisons between this current sexual behavior and what you may have experienced in past relationships. In fact, it is best not to mention prior sexual partners at all. It may add confusion and unnecessary emotions to what should really be an exclusive relationship.

Mind and Body Advice:

- You may be used to being very active during sex, moving your body a lot, stroking with your hands, kissing everything you can. Or, you might like to be still and receptive. Either way is fine, if it works for you, and for your partner. If your mutual activity levels don't seem to be working for good sex, have a conversation and explain what your particular level of activity represents. For example: "I love to lie back and let you have me the way you want. It makes you seem so strong and it makes you very sexy". Or, "I might seem to get carried away when we make love. It's just that you are so important I want to own and possess you".

- You may find that sex becomes much more intense and satisfying when you fantasize. Does this mean that your partner is not enough? Does it mean that you are being unfaithful? In fact, fantasies serve an important purpose during a complex activity like sex. They can help to make you feel strong and capable, or they can make you feel that you deserve to be cared for in the most wonderful ways.

Whatever fantasies you construct, keep and use them regularly for full enjoyment. But if they seem to hamper your drive or performance, get creative and come up with a new scenario, and perhaps some different characters. It would be wise for you to keep your fantasies private – that's what keeps them effective.

- There may be some limitations to your sexual enjoyment due to the state of your body. Certain sexual positions or activities may be difficult because of back pain, hip discomfort, sensitive skin or a need for lubrication. It is best to make your adaptations as naturally as possible – respect the sexual positions that don't hurt, use ointment or medications to treat skin that may have received some intense handling, and use lubrication freely and routinely. As much as possible try to keep your limitations private. If they do come into discussion it is best to appear in charge and matter of fact. Avoid the impression that whatever is going on is permanent – this allows you both to be hopeful and respectful each time you have sex.

- Remember that with sex, timing and circumstances are very important. If you both have active and busy days you may be too tired to have sex when you go to bed. Also, the effects of alcohol may be greater now than when you were younger. If you find your sexual frequency is less than you think it should be a frank discussion of your lifestyle will be helpful. Whether you decide to have sex in the mornings, or to enjoy a glass of wine after sex, discussions will lead to practical changes and greater ability to discuss what is working and what is not.

To sum up: Sexual behavior with your new and special person should be slow, comfortable and exclusive to the two of you. Further, it should take into account emotional, physical and circumstantial factors. Full discussion, acting strong and being hopeful can make any sexual interaction satisfying and fulfilling for both of you.

RELIGIOUS BELIEFS

May Answer Your Prayers

Finding a companion or spouse involves the practice of *searching*, of *hoping*, of having *faith* and of being open to *acceptance*. The nature of your search for someone special has been more religious that you might have realized.

Searching is really an effort to find someone that will care for you, who will be there when you need them, who you can trust and who will be strong enough to travel with you through life.

Hoping that your search will be successful is what enables you to go out with friends time after time, to take part in different social situations, and to give out your name and phone number to stranger after stranger.

Having *faith* allows you to believe there is someone out there who is looking as hard for you as you are for them. It says that someone exists who thinks like you do, who likes what you do, and who wants what's best for you.

Being open to *acceptance* means saying to yourself that you are a good person, that you deserve someone special and that you will find them no matter how long it takes.

Searching, *hoping*, having *faith* and being open to *acceptance* – these are the basic principles of most religious faiths. Does this mean that it is easier to find someone if you are religious? It certainly might be. If your religious experience and life have helped you to feel secure; if your religious community has helped you

HOW SENIORS CAN FIND COMPANIONSHIP OR MARRIAGE

feel self-respect; if your practice of religion gives you that sense of hope, faith and acceptance – then you have a built-in advantage in your search for a partner.

Do you have to "find religion" to get yourself a companion or a spouse? It certainly helps. Use what you have gained from your formal religious background, or become "religious" about using the strategies and suggestions that you are reading about in YOU DON'T HAVE TO LIVE ALONE.

AMEN!

HOBBIES AND INTERESTS

Make a Pastime a Findtime

You know what your hobbies were – the activities that you did with your "extra time", when you didn't have to be at work, when you had a break from raising your children, when you wanted to do something just for you. These hobby and interest activities were really treasured by you – you protected their time and often poured scarce resources into their maintenance. You needed them because they offered a break from all the things you had to do.

At this point in your life your involvement in hobbies or interests is either much greater than ever (you have more free time, perhaps more discretionary income and a growing need to feel worthwhile) or much less than ever (your hobby mates may have drifted away, you need your money for more basic things and there may be a sense that the activities are no longer fulfilling).

As your priority now is to find a significant companion or spouse it is time to make current interests (or hobbies) help you toward that goal. Here's how:

Pick activities that reflect your best qualities and that are likely to attract others with the same qualities.

> Example – You love dogs and wouldn't dream of being with some-
> one who didn't share this same love. So become a volunteer in an
> animal shelter, walk dogs for adoption or get active in fundraising for
> an animal society. This will put you in close contact on a regular basis
> with people you will want to get to know. This time will be of even
> greater value since you'll be with the animals you love. In turn, the

How Seniors Can Find Companionship or Marriage

dogs will give you the energy and persistence to find someone special sooner than later.

Example – You know it is important to keep your mind active and stimulated. Your partner in life must also be dedicated to learning and ongoing mental challenges. Consider attending discussion groups, courses, and lectures. In these settings your ears could be educated while your eyes would be searching for that someone special.

As in the examples above, your hobbies or interests emphasize enjoyable time and desirable qualities. In addition, there are significant numbers of people involved and there is the constant addition of fresh faces.

All of this, taken together, increases the chances of finding a partner while also providing enjoyment for you. Hobbies can be fun and good for you too!

You Don't Have to Live Alone

YOUR WORKPLACE

An Opportunity Place

Work and romance seem worlds apart. Work you have to do; romance you want to do. Work you get paid for; romance is free. Work can use up your energy; romance renews it. Work is scheduled; romance is spontaneous.

And yet, work might be the place for you to discover someone who could be in your life forever. How might this happen? By making your work *work for you*, instead of the other way around.

Though you might think negatively about a situation where you have to be for a certain number of hours every day, it is also true that those working hours provide lots of opportunity for someone to notice you and to want to get to know you.

It also gives you the opportunity to assess someone's personal qualities on a dependable basis – you know where they will be, and when. You can watch how they interact with others and whether they seem friendly or approachable.

If you work in a situation that you don't feel positive about, try not to let that contaminate your potential feelings about others who work there. Socializing outside of work with your coworkers will help you overcome this.

Another positive factor of work is that a group of coworkers has gotten to know you well in a situation that binds you together. They know what you like and what you hate. They hear about your social times outside of work, who you liked and who acted like a jerk. What better group to fix you up with a friend or family member. It's up to you to ask them to do it.

What's especially important for you is to use work as an opportunity for attachment, not as an activity that keeps you unattached.

SEEING AND HEARING

Making Sense of Your Senses

When you decide it's time to find a permanent partner, you go into "search mode" to find the best one as soon as possible. Searching involves seeing and hearing. These two sensory areas can be affected by increasing age. Understanding the roles that the eyes and ears play in your search will be a big advantage to you.

A good way to think about the eyes and ears is that they help you sort out and select who would be best for you; who would feel the best and who you would trust to give you the best care. Initially, sorting this out is done by your eyes – who looks attractive, who dresses well, who has a good way of "taking up space". Your eyes scan all of this, quickly at first with glances, then moving on to longer gazing and staring. You will measure and compare what you see with what you have come to desire – through experience and fantasy.

After your eyes have begun their "sorting out", your ears will do their part to complete the job. This involves getting close enough to hear what this potentially special person has to say – about themselves and their availability. Is the voice quality soothing? Are the words clear and strong? Are emotions expressed directly and consistently?

Clearly then, your eyes and ears have special and important roles to play in the way you select a partner. But is there more you should know? What is often overlooked is the role that your eyes and ears play in how your partner may select you.

How Seniors Can Find Companionship or Marriage

You should be aware that while you are engaged in conversation with this new person, they will be very aware of your eyes – do you look straight at them; do your eyes maintain their gaze, direct and unwavering; do you use your eyes effectively to show emotion, by narrowing or widening them.

To best show off the positive qualities of your eyes, you need to draw your special person in – by using effective eye makeup and wearing glasses that are complimentary. In your initial meetings do not wear sunglasses!

With regard to your ears and hearing you'll be making your impression by how you respond to what the other person is saying. You need good hearing for this. If your hearing is diminishing get a hearing aid quickly! Not only will you hear what you need to but your potential partner will also be pleased that your responses complement their spoken messages.

To sum up: your vision will set things up and your hearing will seal the deal.

FOOD AND YOUR WEIGHT

Loving, then Losing

When you are trying to get into a new relationship you need all the confidence you can have. Unfortunately, feeling confident is not always completely your choice. In part it may be dependent on what someone important may be thinking of you.

You and I know that a major loss of confidence occurs if you think that you are overweight, and, if others think you are overweight as well. Of course the problem with overweight is its connection to eating. It's too bad that something as pleasurable as eating should be linked to something as problematic as your weight. But if being overweight feels bad, not eating feels worse.

I am not advocating being overweight, but I am advocating keeping your priorities straight as you plan to get into a new relationship. You will seem most attractive if you seem strong and comfortable. If you are overweight at the present time – don't stop eating! Your enjoyment of food can be a very endearing quality. It shows that you love living and taking the best that life has to offer. What you don't want to do is apologize for eating or how you look; don't qualify your appearance. If you don't like how you look at present, keep it to yourself.

Once your new relationship is well on its way, once your new partner has grown to love your basic self – that's the time to slowly and surely lose weight. You'll feel loved and confident. This is the best basis for changing your eating habits. It will seem like an extension of your happiness rather than a deprivation of food.

Keep your priorities straight! Eat, then love, then lose weight.

How Seniors Can Find Companionship or Marriage

PERSONAL GEOGRAPHY

Where Love Lives

Personal geography is how you should think about finding a lifelong partner. Big city, small town – where do you have the best chance of meeting someone? If you are asking yourself these questions, it may be that you need more understanding of some basic issues about finding yourself a relationship.

Searching for a partner is like throwing a hook into a pond of goldfish. Your hook will only bring up one fish, but that fish will look very special as you swing it toward you. It won't matter if it's a big pond with a few fish or a little pond with thousands of fish.

In your personal geography, where you spend most of your time becomes the "pond" that you get to know and where you get known in return. This is where you can learn the details of the social life there and who is available.

By keeping your geography simple you avoid the sense that you are always looking in the wrong place (that the fish are biting in the next pond). By "staying put", you keep yourself calmer and less stressed.

Like expertly baiting a hook, you can perfect the signals that you send out (that you are available, that you have a lot of care and love to give, and that you are strong enough to give it well and consistently).

These signals will attract the person you are looking for, and they will be caught. You can then remove the hook, throw away your fishing pole and settle down happily, with your catch, in your little corner of the world.

How Seniors Can Find Companionship or Marriage

COMMUNICATING

Simple Rules Apply

How you communicate is very important in both finding and keeping a meaningful relationship. When you are looking to attract someone special, remember the following:

First, your communications (to yourself or the other person) should:
Generate Interest - "this person seems interested in me", "it seems that they are available", "they appear physically attractive", "we seem to share the same views".

Second, your communications must:
Maintain Interest – "they called when they said they would", "our conversations keep expanding", "I'm constantly learning more about you", "there is much mention of future time together".

To achieve these levels of interest your communication should follow a few simple rules:

1 – Ask as many questions as you want (that's a basic way of getting to know someone) but make many statements as well (it will be reassuring to think that you know a lot and speak with confidence).

2 – Use the person's name a lot (a sure way for them to feel special).

3 – After each conversation take a few minutes to write down names, situations, and details you have gathered and use them in your subsequent contacts (a sure indication that you pay attention and know what's important to this person).

4 – Keep any apologies or qualifications to a minimum (they are a way to keep yourself calm but could make you appear unsure of yourself).

5 – Make as few references as possible to prior relationships (your new person wants to feel exclusive).

It might seem unusual to make "rules" about communicating, but they will help make your search for a romantic partner sure and successful.

PERSONAL HABITS

An Opportunity for Closeness

So you've been biting your nails for a long time. So you curl your hair when you're preoccupied. So you like to sleep hugging your pillow. Is this a problem?

Habits like these have become part of your personal life, but they may cause problems once you add an important someone to that personal life. They may have trouble understanding what the habits are about, or why you seem to need them. They may be reluctant to openly question or criticize you. Or, they may introduce their own collection of habits.

Whether it's one or both of you with the habits, it's good to have a general sense of why they're there and a strategy to deal with them in your new relationship.

Remember this: habits exist for a reason. They are an attempt to make you feel better. Often that backfires. For example you might bite your nails to have something to do with your fingers and mouth, or to serve as a stress reliever. However, realizing how it looks, or seeing the destructive effects on your nails, you may be embarrassed or be self-critical. Habits are a complex behavior and usually have some negative feelings attached to them.

When you meet someone, seeing or being seen with habits can raise some questions about maturity or emotional comfort. If your new person has habits it is best to talk about them if the person brings them up. If they say, "You may have noticed I crack my knuckles. I hope that doesn't bother you". Your best response would be, "I did notice and you must do it because it feels good to you". That lets the other person feel that you are able to talk about this sort of thing in an understanding and mature way.

_____ **61** _____

It will surely give them the confidence to bring it up again if necessary or to bring up something else they may feel awkward about.

If you feel that one of your habits is obvious or is being perceived negatively, be direct and say something like, "I'm sure you've noticed that I bite my nails. It's a habit I'm in charge of and might decide to stop some day". This portrays you as candid and strong, and opens up any further discussion with your partner in a natural way.

Dealing successfully about habits with your partner will definitely be habit-forming!

MEMORY PROBLEMS

Fix the Forgetting

If you suspect you are having memory problems it can cause you great concern. After all, the last thing you need as you are seriously looking for a long term companion is a breakdown of your mental faculties. It is because you depend so on your memory that any problems in that area really sets off alarm bells.

You need a dependable memory for three phases of the new relationship:

> *1- Meeting and greeting your new companion*
> *2- Forming and strengthening the new relationship*
> *3- Maintaining and settling into your life together*

A few words about each phase will help you use your memory to its best advantage:

> 1 – *Meeting and greeting* – When you are being introduced to someone you could very well have a high level of anxiety. This is caused by the "what if" question, "What if I can't remember his/her name?" In other words you cause your own anxiety because of how much you want things to go smoothly. Understanding this may help a lot, to the point where, realizing you've forgotten the person's name, you can say, "Please tell me your name again so I can remember it easily". This way you are not saying you've forgotten but rather are emphasizing the new person's importance.

2 – *Forming and strengthening the new relationship* – As you get to know your new partner there will be shared experiences and new conversations. All of this represents a large amount of information to sort out and remember. You may experience times of forgetfulness as all of this information is new. This could be in the form of "blanking out", or an "it's on the tip of my tongue" feeling. What's important is to get past this quickly, and without giving your partner a sense that you feel impaired. A good way to handle this type of memory issue is to say something like, "We're getting to know so much about each other. Refresh my mind about ......". Again, you appear strong and seem to be thinking positively about your relationship, not worried about losing a memory.

3 – *Maintaining and settling into your life together* – Once you've become a settled couple you become subject to all the positives and negatives of everyday living. Some memory loss might occur at times when there is a lot going on or when you haven't paid as much attention to something as your partner has. Slips of memory or even major forgetting of past events, can be handled so that they don't seem to represent a larger problem. Remember, do not bring up memory loss that your partner may not be aware of, and, if they are aware, say something like, "It's good that when one of us forgets the other can make up for it". This keeps memory loss in its proper place: something that makes sense and that can add to the richness of your life together.

You Don't Have to Live Alone

POLITICS AND PERSONAL VIEWS

Discussing them Wisely

When you talk politics or speak about your personal views you do it for two reasons: to make yourself feel good about what you believe and to make yourself feel important by convincing someone else that your positions are right.

So this kind of talk is really you-centered and may have to be handled carefully when you meet your new partner. A good rule is to hold your own opinions and be primarily responsive to what your new person is saying. It should become obvious fairly soon if they seem to have strong opinions. What you should watch for is how intensely they feel and whether they seem to want your agreement.

Let's first consider the very intense person. Examples might be: "Me, my dad and his dad before him have all been die-hard Republicans" or, "I'm sorry, but I think the Government should do much more for the homeless".

When you encounter this level of intensity in your first interactions together, it is best not to agree or disagree but rather to acknowledge how strongly the person feels. When your first response is something like, "I can tell you really have a strong belief in what you are saying", that calms things down a bit for the other person. They are then in a better position to either ask you calmly about your views or even to move on to some other topic of conversation.

Your potential partner's intent may seem to be to convince you of a particular position. As in: "You have to agree, this President just loves to raise our taxes" or, "I know you think assisted suicide is wrong".

How Seniors Can Find Companionship or Marriage

Pressed to agree or disagree, you want to make a response that indicates you are interested and listening. If it happens that you do agree with what the person is saying, you might say something like, "I feel just like you, and I like the way you express it". If you feel total disagreement you might say, "I can see you've given this a lot of thought, but I'll need time to talk to you more about it".

Politics and personal views have the potential to make your relationship both interesting and significant. That will happen over time and in a lot of conversations between you. It is in the beginning of your time together that these areas of opinion have to be handled wisely, and with patience.

You Don't Have to Live Alone

MORALS

Share and Shape

By this time in your life you have a pretty good set of morals in place. You have tried to live by them when you've been in relationships, in dealing with friends and, perhaps, as you have raised children. In fact, morals have served as a very basic support for your life.

As you think about finding and starting a new relationship you will rely upon those morals. They will help you keep things clear and make decisions. When you meet someone there will be opportunities to assess their morality as well.

At first, social situations will reveal a lot. Do they call when they say they will? That will give you clues about their honesty. Do they apologize if you are kept waiting? That says something about their awareness of hurting someone's feelings.

As things develop between you there will be exposure to your family. Does your partner recognize their importance to you? This says a lot about how much they think about your comfort. When you talk about parenting issues that you are or have been involved with is there agreement about what represents good or bad behavior? This is a basic reflection of someone's morality.

Later, as living together increases personal and physical intimacy, are you being treated respectfully and with an awareness of what feels good or what is hurtful? It is in this phase of your relationship that you and your partner's morals should be similar and mutually supportive.

How Seniors Can Find Companionship or Marriage

What can you do if you realize there is a difference in your morals and those of the person you hope to share your life with? What's most important is realizing it is never too late to change someone's sense of morality.

At some level your significant other will probably know when they are doing or saying something morally "wrong". It's a fact that someone with emotional leverage (like you) is most able to change that behavior.

This is what you do: Be strong, clear, brief and to the point about what you say. Here are some examples:

>Your partner is not calling when they say they will. You say, "It's best for both of us if you call when you say you will. Please do that".

>There is developing resistance to visiting your parents. You say, "Seeing my parents is part of sharing my life. Doing it with me will be good for both of us".

>Your partner has started to stay up after you've gone to bed. You say, "Bedtime is important in our relationship. It is not a good time to be separated".

By being clear about your sense of morality, and acting upon it you will help assure a good standard in your new relationship. Further, your approach will encourage your partner to confront you if there seems to be something wrong with your own morals. After all, morality should work both ways.

SHARING

To Give and to Take

You have been thinking to yourself, and telling friends, how you want to "share your life" with someone.

I congratulate you for being so wise. What you have wanted - sharing - represents the very best aspect of a significant relationship.

Sharing is the most important force in your life. If you are a good "sharer" you will be very attractive to someone very special. Since sharing means both giving and getting at the same time, it feels very good to both you and your partner.

Let's look at one example of sharing to see its importance: You are just getting into what you hope will be a long term relationship. Deciding to bring this person closer, you have invited them for dinner.

During a prior discussion, you learned how much this important person enjoys Italian food. They casually "shared" that with you at a moment of closeness. They "gave" you this information because it felt good to talk about food that tasted good. You gladly "took" this information because it allowed you to feel good too. This important "sharing" stayed with both of you over time and gave you a close feeling. Even when you were apart, any exposure to Italian food – in the supermarket, in TV advertising, eating a pizza – increased your feeling of closeness at a deep level. The "sharing" about Italian food became one of the many threads pulling you closer together.

When you made your dinner invitation you said you would make something special. Of course what you are planning to serve is the great lasagna recipe you are so proud of. This will be a wonderful evening – you will build on a process of "sharing" that started with the first discussion of Italian food.

This is only one example of sharing, but it has all the elements that you need to know, and use, to bring someone close, and keep them close. Sharing is giving and sharing is taking. Sharing occurs at a specific point in time, but becomes an ongoing force to keep you falling in love.

COMPARING

To Get and be the Best

It is impossible to assess the value of something that belongs to you unless you compare it with "others". The problem with comparing is that it takes energy, it sets you up for possible disappointment and the "others" that you are comparing with may be numerous or difficult to assess.

In looking for a companion, or mate, the comparison issue could give you trouble. Let's see how this works so that you can do your comparing as comfortably as possible.

Once you've started a relationship with someone it may seem unfair or even unfaithful to compare them with others. However, comparison is inevitable and often has positive results. If your new companion has a big belly, you will be comparing them with others who also have big bellies or to those with no bellies at all. By comparing this way you get a better sense of how much you want to make an issue of your partner's physical shape.

As you do this comparing it would be best to keep it to yourself. If your partner sees you looking at someone else and suspects you are doing a comparison, they may say, "Do you think that guy looks in better shape than me?" or, "You probably think that girl over there looks young". The best answers are neutral, accompanied by reassurance: "I think your shape is just great and that's what counts" and, "You're the girl whose looks I fell in love with".

Of course if it is obvious to you that there is some comparison concerning you going on, then you can be smart and do something about what is being compared:

How Seniors Can Find Companionship or Marriage

Lose weight and get in better shape, or make sure your makeup and grooming are doing the most for your best features.

Although comparing is very normal in a relationship you want to do it wisely and constructively. You want the best and this is one important way of feeling you have it or helping you get it.

WHERE TO LOOK

It's All about You

"**W**here do I look?" …… I know you've asked yourself that question many times. It's not an easy question because you're likely asking it when you really want to meet someone or when you've just been someplace where no one seemed suitable. It's not an easy question because you're not sure that there really is an answer.

The question of where to look becomes even more difficult because even if you knew where to look, so many others are also looking that your own chances of finding someone special seem few.

Should you go to socials? Mixers? Bars? Can you really feel special when so many other singles are present? Does "looking" take away the magic of meeting someone you can love?

Isn't there something to the idea of "destiny" leading you or being "made for each other"?

The good news is that these questions can be answered simply, and in ways that will make the search for your partner not only rewarding, but enjoyable as well.

The first thing to remember is that you are most likely to meet that special person when you are feeling the most comfortable. This will allow you to send out the strongest signals – of interest and availability. So "where to look" means in places where you like the surroundings (food served, music played and types of people present).

Secondly, only look in situations that reflect your own personal interests. Again this maximizes your comfort, but also increases the odds of finding like-minded companionship.

So "where to look" means in places where you are familiar with the prevailing activities (bicycling, modern art galleries, bird watching, contra-dancing, etc.)

As you follow my advice, the "where do I look" question will change to "how do I make a choice".

MEETING EXPECTATIONS

Make it Happen

If you're going to be spending the rest of your life with someone you surely want them to meet your expectations. You'll want them to appreciate the things in life that you do; you'll want them to have some idea of what life has meant for you; you'll want them to know what you need and to make an effort to give it to you. In addition, you can be sure that they will have the same expectations of you.

How can expectations like these be met? How long might it take? How can you know if it's happening the way that it should?

In YOU DON'T HAVE TO LIVE ALONE you have been reading about the most crucial ingredient in a successful new relationship – effective communication.

If you are smart with your communications, expectations will be met and you will feel you are in a rewarding relationship.

Let's consider together how to be smart with these communications:

> When talking about your expectations *use direct, everyday language* ("I've noticed how you are considerate of people's feelings. I'm looking forward to being with someone who is like that").

> *Don't compare your expectations* in this relationship to failed expectations in prior relationships ("I hope you enjoy romantic dinners together. That wasn't the case with other people I've been with").

If the new person you are seeing lets you down with regard to your expectations say something that gets your point across *without appearing hurt or needy yourself* ("I know our relationship would be a lot better for you if you returned my calls more quickly").

You certainly have expectations now, and you will probably develop more as you get involved with a new partner. Handling them in a smart way will deliver the most expectations from your relationship.

FATE OR CIRCUMSTANCE

A Role for Each

You and I know that your primary goal is to meet the person who can be a significant companion or spouse.

But if I asked you whether it should be fate or circumstance that helps you find this person, which would you choose? Most likely you would pick fate. That's because you want your relationship to be special, and fate seems more special than circumstance.

Fate has qualities that seem to apply to romance especially. There is something magical and unpredictable about fate. There is a sense that it can work very powerfully for you. And most of all, there is the implication that some "force" or "power" is in charge of making sure that things work in your favor. How can you beat that?

Well, circumstance doesn't seem able to beat that. Circumstance seems emotionless. It seems neutral toward you. And it seems to work by you manipulating it.

So do you depend on magical fate or plain old circumstance to help you in your search? Ideally you use the best of both.

> Consider this example: There is a weekly singles dance in your community where there is a DJ, good food, inexpensive drinks and a steady supply of newcomers. In addition, it is held on Friday nights, which works for you since you have friends who are usually available to go then. These are all circumstances – they are predictable, dependable and you can make the decision to use them. They may not be magical but they can tilt things in your favor.

By taking advantage of these circumstances you can ensure a comfortable environment, supportive friends and a fair supply of potential partners.

So where does fate come in? It is when one person at the dance seems especially attractive and starts to talk with you. It is when you find you have so many things in common with them. It is when this person wants to be in contact the next day. That's when you can start to think that it "was meant to be" or that you "were made for each other".

You made the circumstances work in your favor and fate did the rest. It was the winning combination.

YOUR LIVING SITUATION

An Extension of You

Meeting your partner can truly be a life-changer. It will bring lots of change for you and your new companion. The changes I'm referring to are with your emotions and your general outlook on life. Those changes will feel good and you can start looking forward to them.

However, to make sure all that happens you may want to consider whether there should be some changes in your living situation. This would be for the purpose of your best success in meeting and keeping a partner.

In the beginning stages of a relationship you should be able to provide privacy and creature comforts to the new person you are spending time with.

If you are living with extended family or grown children you will have to be clear with them about when you will be bringing someone home. Don't hesitate to insist on adjusting schedules or family activities. Emphasize that your privacy with this new person is important and that everyone, including the family, will benefit. By being strong in this way you send a message that you feel good about the new relationship – this reassures everyone and makes their cooperation more likely.

If there are household issues – like demanding pets, broken appliances or general messiness – they need to be taken care of before the person starts visiting regularly.

Your household is an extension of you and your new companion will be attracted to a living situation that is orderly, predictable and comfortable.

As your relationship progresses and your partner becomes a regular part of your living situation – get them integrated as much as possible. Listen to their opinion of what they like or are bothered by, in your usual situation and act upon it.

If they enjoy you cooking for them, encourage them to pick out recipes that you could make. If you hear complaints about how the toilet seat wiggles around, ask if they could pick up some new screws to fix it at the hardware store.

The sooner you can make your living situation comfortable and an extension of your relationship together, the sooner you will have that special person believing they could be a part of it – permanently.

WHO KNOWS YOU'RE LOOKING

The Ones that Matter

Is it better to be a quiet looker or should you advertise your intentions far and wide? Which is more your style, and which is likely to be more successful?

If you've lived your life privately and seriously, it may seem unnatural to discuss your desire for a relationship in a public way. If your ideas about romance emphasize deep feelings and intimate times it may seem inappropriate to tell others what kind of partner you are looking for.

In addition, when you are with friends and hear them talk about "who met who", and "whose relationship didn't work", and how "there's no one out there," it may make you reluctant to join in about your personal desires.

So does looking for someone special need to be a secret search or can you get some support for your efforts? It is a fact that often people have contacts, some have great advice and some would get pleasure seeing you fixed up with a nice person. In fact, the more people you have "working with you" the better the odds that you will find a partner.

Here's how to enlist the aid of others while feeling that you are respecting yourself:

> When you talk about your desire to meet someone *be definite* – not "I want to meet somebody, but it seems such a hassle", but rather "Meeting a special person is now my first priority".

Emphasize how *the person you meet will be very lucky* – not "I don't want to spend any more lonely nights", but rather "The person who gets me will thank their lucky stars!"

Save your serious requests for names and introductions from those who *seem to be associated with good relationships themselves* – by actually being in them or through social or family associations.

In all these ways you will maximize your chances of meeting the person you are looking for. You will also have developed a group of people who will stay close to you – because you are appreciative of them and because they are appreciative of you – after all, you have allowed them into a very important part of your life and seemed strong and attractive in the process.

REJECTION

Making it Positive

You can't really prepare yourself for rejection. You understand that it has to be part of a serious search for a companion or spouse, but when it happens it's a blow. You have the inevitable thoughts about whether you did something wrong, whether you were not considered attractive, and whether or not it's all worth it. Then you might go through the angry thoughts about the other person's lack of consideration, and that they probably wouldn't have been the right person anyway.

These are the reactions that happen inside you. You then have to decide whether to keep it all private or to let others know what happened. Sometimes you have no choice. Your friends or family may know you've been seeing someone and you may have kept them informed about how the relationship was progressing.

What is the best way to handle rejection? I want you to notice my use of the word "handle". I didn't say "get past it" because you want to handle a rejection and turn it into something that can offer opportunities, provide understanding and generally be a positive step along the road to love.

These are the steps you can take as you "handle" what seems to be a rejection:

- Don't say anything to anybody until you have a chance to *collect your thoughts*.

- Try to *feel sorry for the other person* for giving up the opportunity to get some really good care.

HOW SENIORS CAN FIND COMPANIONSHIP OR MARRIAGE

- Think back and decide whether there were any *earlier indications of rejection* that you either didn't recognize or ignored.

- Finally, tell anyone you want to, or have to, what happened. In this discussion indicate that you *understand* how it all made sense, that you are *ready to move* into a new relationship and that you are *doing well*.

By doing these things you will be more prepared for the future, and will maintain the support and interest of your friends. The rejection will become a distant memory overshadowed by great hope – and hope can make you a very attractive person.

SOMEONE TO TAKE CARE OF YOU

Getting and Giving Together

"The best care is not what you get, but what you give".

This great truth is the basis for finding, and keeping, a truly good caregiver for yourself. When you are alone, when you crave physical contact, when you want to laugh or share a meal – these are all situations where you want someone to take care of you.

You may fantasize about how this would be, and how good it would feel. But wait! Let's take a close look at these care situations that involve a significant partner:

> *Not being alone* – If someone is with you they also are not alone. You are a presence in their life just as they are in yours. You are taking care of each other just by being available to each other.

> *Having physical contact* – At those times when your partner is touching, holding or hugging you, it is your body that makes that possible. Your responsive touch and hugs keep the interaction going. Physical contact requires and provides for two bodies.

> *When you laugh together* – It's nice to have an amusing person around; it feels good to laugh. However, it is your laughter that gives your partner a sense of accomplishment, and the desire to keep you laughing. The audience and the performer become united.

HOW SENIORS CAN FIND COMPANIONSHIP OR MARRIAGE

When you share a meal – Even as you enjoy the taste of your food and the warmth of the wine you are making appreciative comments to your companion. This increases the pleasure of the meal for them and makes them a more interactive eating partner. The meal gets better and better for both of you.

So when you talk about how you are looking for someone to take care of you, you are talking about so much more: You are saying that you understand how much is necessary in a relationship. You are saying that you are strong enough to provide your care contribution to being a couple. Most of all you are saying that the "great truth" about care is energizing you to find the person who will get loads of care themselves by giving it to you.

Both of you will be fortunate indeed!

GETTING ADVICE

You Decide its Value

Advice about relationships is tricky. Having your pride, you may not feel like asking about something so personal. You may feel awkward if advice is offered by someone you don't feel that close to. You may not know who to ask for advice and it may seem that a lot of advice that is offered is worthless. Yet people love to give advice and you know that you are always looking for ideas or suggestions that will help you find your partner.

Even the word "advice" is obviously well-intended but may not in fact be helpful. How do you get truly helpful advice in a way that keeps you comfortable and yet lets you feel in charge of things?

Here is what I suggest:

> -When you ask someone for advice *think about it in advance* and *keep your questions as specific* as possible: "I've been thinking about going to Authors' Discussion Night on Wednesday evening. Do you think I'd like the people who show up there?" This allows you to get practical information you can use and minimizes any other advice which may confuse things.

> - Be *selective about who you are asking* for advice. Don't waste your time asking the neighbor who has been in and out of relationships about how to meet someone for the long term. Asking advice from the "wrong people" will probably get you the "wrong advice".

How Seniors Can Find Companionship or Marriage

- When someone gives you *unsolicited advice,* don't feel that you have to engage them in a long discussion.

Most times people offer advice because it makes them feel helpful and important. That doesn't make it bad advice, but it also doesn't insure that it is good advice either. In these situations it is helpful to have a reply that doesn't take too much time or energy and leaves you feeling in charge: "I really appreciate your interest. Let me get back to you when I have more time".

Advice can be as great as the person who gives it and as great as the person who takes it. You want to make it work for you both ways.

WATCHING OTHER COUPLES

Almost Like Being There

That couple over there…. What are they doing? What are they to each other? How do they feel about each other? These are all thoughts that you have when you are out in social situations. It's as if couples have a magnetic cloud around them that attracts your attention. Why spend so much energy watching what you want so much yourself? There are good reasons you do this, but it can be a difficult process.

The major reason you watch other couples is that it's the next best thing to being a part of the couple yourself. You become part of their interaction. If hands are held, if bodies are close, if tender gazes are exchanged, you are practically there with them.

Another important reason is that by watching people you may learn something new, something you may use yourself someday. After all, if those two people are a couple they must be doing something right.

Another, less obvious reason for couple-watching is that it provides you the opportunity to compete with the person of your same sex. You can compare the way that gal touches her companion with the way you have learned to touch a man. You can compare how the two of them pay attention to each other versus how you would do it. Do they pick up each other's signals? Do they miss any cues?

All these reasons for watching are important to keep in mind because another feature of couple-watching is its ability to make you feel uneasy or sad. It's nice to feel a part of that couple you have been watching, but once they are out of sight you may experience a loss.

HOW SENIORS CAN FIND COMPANIONSHIP OR MARRIAGE

It's good to learn from and compare what other couples do, but what about your opportunity to put this into practice? If there is no opportunity right now you're not going to feel so great.

So when you find yourself watching other couples remember that you are doing it for very good reasons. Rather than look away observe what is happening, learn some new tricks and feel, by comparison, that you have lot to offer someone yourself.

THE ONES THAT DON'T WORK OUT

What that Really Means

When a relationship doesn't work out for you, how do you get past it? You dated the guy for four months, shared meals, met his children, and were intimate with him. You really thought things were going well. Then he started making excuses for his time and finally stopped calling or responding to your calls.

What YOU DON'T HAVE TO LIVE ALONE wants to accomplish is getting you past this experience without feeling that it was your fault or losing hope about forming a new relationship.

When a relationship ends unhappily, you may find yourself going over incidents or interactions in your mind. It may seem that you are trying to make sense of what happened, but a more significant purpose is to hang on to the person you have just lost.

Therefore it is very important to move on to another potential partner as soon as possible.

There may also be a sense that somehow it was your fault; that things would have worked out if you did something differently. This is a more common feeling when someone takes a relationship away from you rather than you ending it yourself. Feeling that you have done something wrong or that you were bad, is very handicapping. It can make your next effort to meet someone much more difficult.

Finally, a breakup can leave you feeling vulnerable. This is not a good way to proceed. What will restore your sense of being strong is knowing what you have

How Seniors Can Find Companionship or Marriage

to offer. Think to yourself and tell friends that the person you broke up with lost a valuable opportunity; that your next companion will be very lucky indeed.

Finding a companion or spouse takes a lot of hard work and exposes you emotionally. When you do things with strength and understanding, the odds of forming a successful relationship are very much in your favor. It can be reassuring to know that the "ones who get away" are not the ones you would want to keep.

DOES ATTRACTIVENESS HELP

Only in the Complete Sense

Before you go out in public some of your most significant moments are spent in front of the mirror. You are assessing your own attractiveness. Or, to be more precise, you are assessing how another might assess your attractiveness. The more important issue, however, is whether you think you will be pursued, or rejected, based on how attractive you look.

Good relationships are dependent on far more than physical attractiveness. Actually, being very beautiful or handsome can be a handicap in that it may lead to expectations that are not met. Such things as generosity, strength and availability are what really attract others. These traits are revealed over an extended period of time. So true attraction, contrary to popular belief, is not something that occurs in the moment.

What about the time in front of the mirror? Is it really necessary? What's important is that you meet some basic standards of physical attractiveness. These include: how you groom your skin and hair, how you make your mouth smile, and how you direct your eyes. Your clothing should generally reflect the standards of the time, perhaps with some special flourish that you consider unique. An alluring scent attracts as well. All this makes it more likely that someone will want to stay around and get to know you over time. It is over time that your complete attractiveness will become more and more apparent. Attractiveness, then, is not a mirror thing. It is a "who you really are" thing.

As your relationship extends over time and your partner keeps saying, "I find you very attractive", you'll know that you are succeeding in making things work for a happy future together.

USING TODAY'S TECHNOLOGY

Wisely and Selectively

In the rapidly evolving world of technology, romance remains the same as it always has been. As you look to find a long-term partner, it is important to follow the customs of romance while using the best of technology to assist you. Of course this implies that you avoid the worst of technology which may work against you.

Everything from telephones, to electronics, to household appliances, has been technologically upgraded to make things faster, easier and even more fun. As you meet and interact with a new person you need to know how the use of this technology can benefit a new relationship.

Let's consider the cell phone, as its use is important in establishing effective communication. When you meet someone who seems interesting, you will probably exchange phone numbers with them.

Instead of writing the number down like people used to, you are now more likely to enter it into your phone. That's well and good but a nice twist would be to hand your phone to your new acquaintance and ask them to enter their number. This immediately makes them a beginning part of your life. They've held your phone, entered their number and seen it on the screen. Every time they call you they'll think of this initial interaction.

Once regular communication has been established it may be tempting to text back and forth, but try to use voicemail when possible. The sound of your voice is an essential part of your communication, probably more important than the actual message.

95

Another device that seems to be everywhere is the MP3 player. This device is certainly wonderful in providing personal audio pleasure but your goal in a good relationship is to have as much mutual pleasure as possible.

Try not to have the ear buds in when you are with your new person. This suggests a barrier to them; that they can't be part of something that you are enjoying. It also makes you feel excluded from any potential interaction. Listen to music or radio together, in your home, or in the car.

Considering other devices that are automatic, remote or programmable, try to remember that there is an advantage to doing things together in a relationship - which doesn't happen if one person takes charge of the TV remote. It's also nice to figure things out together – having a GPS take you everywhere eliminates the fun of helping each other with a map or visible landmarks.

Let me sum up this way: technology is great for making life easier and quicker. You will certainly take advantage of it as you and your partner go through life.

But try not to forget that when things are a challenge, when you choose to do things more slowly together, when you have to talk instead of just pushing buttons, you help to maintain closeness and a sense of accomplishment together.

LEARNING FROM MISTAKES

Signals Make it Easy

Mistakes, although unpleasant, present a valuable way of learning what not to do. As you look for, and then develop a relationship with someone, mistakes will be made by both of you. Some will be more serious than others, but almost all can be undone. Most people are aware when mistakes are made that jeopardize their sense of comfort. They will send out signals that are meant to have the mistakes corrected. If the signals are picked up the relationship can be repaired.

One of the most difficult things to decide when you are starting a new relationship, is how much to ask about the other person's life before you met them. You would like to know as much as possible because that would make you feel close. But there may be a lot that your partner is not ready to share.

If you make the mistake of asking too much, you are likely to get a signal to stop or slow down a bit. This signal may be an obvious upset mood, an effort to switch the conversation, or an angry statement about what you are doing. You learn from this mistake because it is emotionally intense and because the signals are clear. Ideally you take what you learn from the mistake and try to maintain a good relationship. A few words that can help: "I can see I've upset you. When you feel ready to share some more of your life with me you can be sure I'll be glad to listen".

Other common mistakes in the beginning phases of your relationship will involve sex, adult children and the process of spending more time with each other. Whichever of you has made a mistake in these areas, you can both benefit by handling it properly. This should involve *being sensitive to signals of discomfort*, and being wise enough to stop, withdraw, or go more slowly.

If you then *say something that describes what has happened* and *finish off with a hopeful statement,* you will have done a wonderful job of "learning from mistakes". It will actually be both of you who learn no matter who made the mistake. In this way mistakes can lead to a more trusting bond between the two of you.

INTERNET ASSISTANCE

"Search" for Success

The relationship you have with your computer can be very companionable. It glows, plays videos and talks to you. It learns your "favorites" and keeps them available. It can be taken with you or accessed when you are separated. It is especially good at searching for what you seem to need and presenting it to you in stimulating ways.

There is a special type of computer search you've heard about, and you may have even tried – the search for a good companion. As you know, there are websites dedicated to finding you a match. Typically they promise to connect you with one of their thousands of members who, like yourself, are looking for companionship.

Is it a good idea to use one of these services? The answer is a qualified "yes". You are smart to use it for what it can give you, while at the same time remembering its limitations. Think of this type of website like going to a dance. There is a population of singles who are there for the same reason you are. You all want to dance but you have to decide who you want to dance with more than once and who you would like to spend time with after the dance is over. Just like the people you meet at a dance, the contacts provided by a dating site are only the first step – providing choices. The limitation is that only you, over a period of time, can decide who makes you feel comfortable, who makes you smile and who seems to want to share experiences that feel right to you.

Another internet feature that can encourage a relationship is email. It may begin as casual information sharing and progress to more substantial messages. What's important about a growing email relationship is that it should not take the place of verbal communication. It may seem easier to send out a quick email, but try to talk with spoken words whenever possible. Hearing your potential partner's voice binds you to them and makes them more significant.

Finally, you can use the power of the internet to search for a partner "in all the right places". Knowing where people of similar interests meet, talk, and interact will help you to spend your time most efficiently to meet someone. You need to know that Bridge for Beginners is meeting at St. Catherine's church every Wednesday evening at 6:30 so you can put in your appearance. Perhaps that very special person is sitting at the third table from the end – with the empty seat next to them.

IS BEING SMART IMPORTANT

Brain vs. Heart

I think we agree that you don't want to get into a relationship with a "dummy". That's because a "dummy" wouldn't be able to meet your needs. I'm sorry to use such a nonprofessional term to make my point, but I do so to emphasize how "being smart" in a relationship is often misunderstood and confusing.

When you first meet someone promising, you may try to impress them. If you are having a conversation, it may seem logical to talk smart in order to make that impression. You may use facts or your worldly knowledge to do that.

For example: In one of your first conversations, the subject of movies may come up. To sound smart you find yourself talking about directors, movie stars and old movies.

Your new "potential person" tries to keep up, mentioning movie facts that they know. This conversation may be filled with information but it may lack what is really important – the element of closeness. However, being a "really smart" conversationalist, you then talk about how movies give you a magical feeling, how they make an evening special and how there happens to be a new movie opening this Friday that you think the two of you might enjoy.

Congratulations! You realized that being smart is important but being smart in the right way is more important. To think of it in different terms: Your brain thinks of the words but your heart decides the smart way to use them.

NO PARTNER SADNESS

You Can Make it Go Away

Your mind is wonderful. It has spent many years learning about the world and has tried to adapt to it and protect you as best it could. When you are hurt or shocked, it tries to understand and move on. When you are angered, it tries to react and move on. Its biggest weak spot is the feeling of being unloved by an available and trusted person.

Not having a significant partner creates a deep and ongoing sadness that is always present. It's not that you are always aware of it, but it has the potential to swell up in many circumstances. When you see a couple holding hands, when you see someone who is attractive but unavailable, when you have an empty Saturday evening; that is when the sadness comes.

What to do?

You certainly don't want to read about being sad any longer. You just don't want it to be there. So let's move on!

My intent in presenting YOU DON'T HAVE TO LIVE ALONE is to help you find a long term companion or spouse. However, an important beginning step is to get past the sadness you feel now. That will help to energize you and make you the most attractive you can be.

It's important to understand that sadness makes sense. It is all about loss. If you don't have a partner your mind perceives it as a loss – so it produces sadness. This sadness can be more or less, short or long, depending on how you handle it.

How Seniors Can Find Companionship or Marriage

If you think how bad it hurts, if you think it will never get better, if you think that somehow it's your fault – all these kinds of thoughts make sadness last longer and feel worse than necessary.

So even this basic understanding of how sadness works can help you get past it. Then it is important to fill your mind with ideas, planning, and positive fantasies, and move to the big prize – your Partner! A good way to do this is by reading and re-reading the topics in YOU DON'T HAVE TO LIVE ALONE. As you process them and put them into action, the emotion of sadness will slip further and further away.

IS THIS "THE ONE"

Making Sure

When you make your choice you want it to be the right one. With all the hopes and longing you've had, with all the energy required to meet someone, you don't want to make a mistake.

Finding somebody special means meeting lots of people and doing lots of socializing. You will need to compare and eliminate, winding up with a good choice. Every person you meet will have a question attached to them: Is this "The One"?

Can this lead to doubts and confusion? You bet. This is because as you get to know someone, you get deeper and deeper into their character and traits. They in turn may give a variety of messages to you based on the different ways you present yourself.

Here are some suggestions to help you decide about "The One":

   - Keep a *priority list* that you consult regularly; it may include things like reliability, availability, empathy, common interests, etc.

   - Try to *keep your deliberations to yourself.* Talking to too many others will be confusing – you are the best judge.

   - Once you think you have a serious candidate *stop dating or seeing others.* To really make a final choice you have to have someone in an exclusive position.

Once you have found "The One", you will really love being the "The Two of you".

BEING FIXED UP

Makes Everybody Happy

You know how it works: You made sure your children had nice playmates because it was best for them – it also allowed you to feel reassured. You make sure to take your dog to the vet because that insures his health – it also makes you feel good that you can continue to enjoy a loving pet. So you do for others not just for them, but for yourself as well.

Your friends care about you, and a big reason is because of how you make them feel. If they know you want to meet someone, they have a natural tendency to help. After all, the happier you are, the better friend you can be to them.

You've probably discovered that the friends who try the hardest to "fix you up" are the ones that are in, or have been in, satisfying relationships.

If one of your friends talks about someone they want you to meet, be receptive as you discuss things. Your friend is trying to do something for you so they don't want to see a reaction of rejection or anxiety. In this discussion be sure to give the message, "I know how much you want me to meet somebody".

When the fix-up is offered it is important that you remain in charge of the time frame and circumstances involved: "It will work best for everybody if I get back to you about when this meeting should occur". And, to the candidate: "I want to give this the best chance, so let's talk more about how we should meet".

There may be a situation where your friends have tried many times to fix you up successfully and it hasn't yet happened.

HOW SENIORS CAN FIND COMPANIONSHIP OR MARRIAGE

Rather than imply there may be something lacking in you tell your friends something like, "You know it's important to get it right. I'm learning more what I want for myself all the time".

When it happens that you are fixed up with "Mr./Ms. Right" be prepared for a lot of follow up from the person(s) who fixed you up. They will be naturally curious, but more important they have a vested interest in your ongoing happiness – it adds to their happiness as well.

So you see, when a friend tries to fix you up they are trying to fix themselves up as well.

CHILDREN IN NEW RELATIONSHIPS

Adding to the Love

When you meet your forever partner, you will do things together, develop common interests and generally have a life that enriches each other. One of the qualities that may draw you together is also one that could present a real challenge – the effectiveness of one or both of you as parents.

When you start seeing each other regularly in your home situations it can be very endearing to see your partner act as a loving and effective parent (or grandparent). Helping a teenager with a school project, being generous when money is needed, making time to go to a grandchild's soccer game – these are all evidence of a responsible and giving nature. Discussions about past experiences with children can provide meaningful insights about each other as well.

As your relationship intensifies and you spend more time together, it follows that you will also spend more time with the children. If it's a child who is still dependent, then actual child rearing is something that will become part of your relationship. If the child is living independently, or has a family of their own, you will probably become involved in those extended family situations as well.

How much should you get involved? A good rule is the "fiddle" rule – that is, you allow your partner to have priority if you're with their child, or you insist on your own priority if you're with your child. The actual parent is "first fiddle", the other plays "second fiddle". But like in a good orchestra the non-parent joins in and creates harmony by showing they could be a valuable component of this new

How Seniors Can Find Companionship or Marriage

family and by supporting actions and decisions of the parent. For example, "I can see you have a great relationship with your mom". And, "Your dad is always talking about you".

What about situations where children give signals that they don't welcome the new partner? It's best for the child's parent to respond to negative remarks. They have the most impact, and often what the child is expressing is more about the parent than the parent's new partner. There may be strong feelings that loyalty to a deceased or divorced parent is being transferred to a relative stranger. It also may be a shock to see a parent engaging in activities that they associate with another person.

Some things the parent can say: "I know it's an adjustment to have Dave around so much, but it's an important relationship for me. The better it makes me feel, the better parent I can be for you". And, "Seeing me do all these new things with Marie must seem strange to you. However, they make sense to me and I want you to enjoy me enjoying myself".

Just as children enriched your earlier life so they can enrich the new relationship you develop with your partner.

HANDLING NEGATIVE SITUATIONS

Can Bring You Closer

In a new relationship, a negative situation is one in which you *question whether your partner is right* for you or *circumstances threaten the relationship.* In either case you need to have a plan to understand what is happening and how to deal with it.

Think of a new relationship as a meeting point of two roads. You and your partner have each come down your own road and you meet in this place of romance. What you each bring with you are your own development and experiences. They may seem very similar at first but the more time you spend together the more differences may appear.

For example, when you first met you enjoyed having a coffee together or bringing a sandwich to eat in the park. But as time goes by your partner is insisting that you eat only at upscale restaurants, and, have a full meal there, including dessert. Does this mean that your partner has issues around food or appearances? Can you stay with someone like this?

First, understand that this kind of behavior makes sense in some way. Second, be clear about how it doesn't work well for you. Third, suggest a way of making both of you happy through compromise. You might say something like, "I know it makes you feel good to go out and eat this way but it is not something I like to do a lot. Let's agree to have a meal like this about once a month and decide together where to go".

HOW SENIORS CAN FIND COMPANIONSHIP OR MARRIAGE

As an example of a threatening circumstance: you have begun a relationship with someone who suddenly discovers they have a heart condition. It may require some physical limitation, or medication, or both. How do you maintain the excitement and hope for the future that you both had before?

First, understand how this circumstance is affecting you. In a relationship based on mutual care giving, the possibility that your partner may be weakened seems to put your care at risk. Second, be clear about the fact that this new situation is making you think seriously about how to move ahead together. Third, make a statement that is both strong and hopeful. You might say something like, "This heart situation has certainly been a surprise for both of us. I think it will give us both an opportunity to meet some new challenges and be supportive with each other".

When you turn negative situations into positive solutions your relationship together will become more meaningful. You can continue down the road of love handling future negative situations as they arise.

THE ANIMAL ADVANTAGE

Leashing a Partner

Wouldn't you like a quick and effective way to meet someone while at the same time appearing natural and desirable? Wouldn't it be nice to show a potential partner when you are first meeting them what a tender caregiver you can be? This is all possible and available thanks to the domestic animal kingdom.

The relationship you have with a pet can be a great advantage in your search for a companion or spouse. When you are out and about with your dog, your way of talking to the pooch can attract someone's attention even before they take notice of your physical appearance. Utterances of endearment, strong messages of control – these can be very attractive; just what a special someone would like to experience for themselves.

Once you have attracted someone's attention, and they show interest in a conversation, continue your interaction with doggie, but include the newly interested person in the dialogue. To the animal: "This nice person knows a good dog when they see one" or, to the person: "I have a feeling you enjoy dogs a lot".

After this initial "introduction", be sure to ask the person of interest whether they usually walk in this area, or say very clearly that this is where you like to walk the dog every day. By this point you have developed a conversation of common interests and activities. The rest should flow easily.

Another situation where a pet can be advantageous occurs when you are entertaining someone of interest in your home.

Let's suppose you are the loving owner of a sweet feline. It is smart to use your cat as a partner in your effort to impress your guest. By talking about your pet owner experiences you can clearly convey a picture of responsibility, love and sacrifice – all qualities that a future partner will be happy you possess. In addition the experience of watching you pick up, hug and stroke the purring cat will stir thoughts and fantasies about you that can help you get the relationship you want.

As you know animals were domesticated for many practical reasons. There was also a romantic reason – to find and leash a partner.

ARGUING POSITIVELY

Means Growing Together

The problem with arguing is it makes everything seem so negative. It can make you question your new relationship, or even make you wonder if it really is a relationship. You may even find yourself thinking about other relationships that you've been in where arguing took place.

Coming to a new relationship as a mature adult means having certain standards of behavior. You know what you like and what should be. You're starting with a partner now who also brings their own experiences to the relationship. The potential for disagreement is clear.

When this disagreement becomes significant, then the stage is set for an argument. The stage is also set for an important step forward if the arguing is done in a way that can benefit you both.

Positive arguing is done according to: *how you feel during* the argument, *what you say during* the argument and *what happens after* the argument. Remember, you wouldn't even bother arguing if you didn't think your partner had something positive they could provide for you.

I'm sure you know from years of experience that arguing can produce feelings of being bad and questions of who is really at fault. So be sure about the issues involved and be willing to "fight" for what you think is right. Your partner will have a positive experience just because you will seem so strong and sure of your position. It is when someone wavers or keeps changing their positions that the other person gets more upset.

The words you use during an argument can make a big difference in the outcome for both you and your new partner.

Even though you have both had prior experiences in relationships, don't bring them up when you are arguing with each other. Being exclusive applies to difficult moments as well as close moments. Also, try not to make it seem like the outcome of this argument is going to determine your future together. If one partner feels the relationship is at risk it will only intensify their emotions.

An argument is really of the moment, so when it is over it is best not to reference it. Don't say, "All we do is argue". What you can do positively after you've argued is to give praise to your partner. Do this when it is obvious they have learned from the argument and are trying to do things differently.

A new partner is going to learn a lot about you from what you feel strongly about. Arguments can be positive opportunities to help them do this learning.

RESPECT ME, RESPECT YOURSELF

Helps a Relationship Grow

You've been in the situation many times: It's a crowded Saturday at the mall and a gentlemanly type holds the door for several people behind him. Most go through as if it were an automatic door. But there is one female shopper who smiles at the door-holder and says a distinct, "Thank you".

If these two people happened to be interested in a relationship they would have already made a good start. What had occurred between them was an exchange of respect. The door man showed respect to all the people he held the door for. But only the gal who said thank you returned that respect.

Understanding the basic elements of respect will help you to recognize it and encourage it in your new relationship. Respect means that you think another person is deserving and worthy and you show it by the way you act, or what you say to them. The door holder respected the other shoppers and thought they deserved easy entry. The gal who thanked him appreciated his gesture and then showed him respect with her show of gratitude.

When you meet a prospective partner, be on the lookout for how they show you respect. It could be in the form of being on time when you meet, of trying to accommodate your schedule when you make arrangements to socialize, or by holding a door. It could be apparent when they realize you've said the wrong word but lets it go by, when you indicate you're too tired to be intimate and they graciously back off, or when they complement your guacamole even though it's too salty.

How Seniors Can Find Companionship or Marriage

In addition to realizing that this new partner is respectful of you, you can help build the relationship by how you receive and respond to the respect. Most important, show your recognition of it: "I've noticed that you're always on time". In addition, show how it impacts you: "It's a good feeling knowing you're there when you say you will be". Finally, show your respect in turn: "I think that somebody who is punctual really has it together". Handling respect this way ensures that it will continue to grow between the two of you.

Back and forth, round and round, the mutual dance of respect can become a defining aspect of your relationship.

BEING PRIVATE

Love Hates Publicity

Now that you've decided it's time to get yourself into a meaningful relationship, some things will have to change. In YOU DON'T HAVE TO LIVE ALONE you have been reading about some of these changes. I've talked with you about your friends, about your family, and about society in general – in all these contexts there have been suggestions and ideas about what you can do differently and effectively with these people. They are your "public", and they will always be there.

As much as these people play various roles in your life, their presence in a new relationship may not be ideal. This is because in affairs of the heart privacy is often best. When you first meet someone you learn the most and things move fastest when it is just the two of you.

No distractions means clearer communications. You can both pick up subtle signals from each other that help you navigate the unfamiliar waters of a first meeting. You don't continue talking about a subject when you sense avoidance or discomfort. And you go after subjects that bring on a smile or an air of excitement.

Learning about each other in private immediately gives your relationship a feeling of being special. You can avoid competition from others, or the possibility of interruption that exists in a social setting.

To gain privacy, especially in an initial encounter, may be challenging. There is no established connection yet and you may raise the anxiety of the new person if they are unsure of your intentions. Some things you might say:

HOW SENIORS CAN FIND COMPANIONSHIP OR MARRIAGE

"There is so much going on here that I can't quite listen to you the way I'd like" or, "I have a feeling we could communicate better if there weren't so many interruptions".

As you start to see your new partner more there may be pressure to give up some of your privacy. Friends want to meet each of you and then socialize together. There are more family occasions and it becomes appropriate to bring each other to them. There is also the possibility that in previous relationships your partner never learned the great pleasure of private time.

You want your new relationship to be a forever thing. To help this happen you must make privacy a forever thing.

Whether the two of you are confronting challenges or changes the solutions will come from discussions that are intense, emotional and based on your own experiences. It's best if only the two of you are involved - privately.

YOU DON'T HAVE TO LIVE ALONE

ABSENCE AND YOUR HEART

Presence Makes the Heart Fonder

The absence of someone who cares about you and supports you is not easy. Sometimes it is unavoidable; sometimes it becomes a habit. Looking back you can probably remember the significant absences in your life very well. Whether those absences were many or few you want a new relationship where the person you love is very available.

It is important to lay the groundwork for a "presence relationship" as early as possible. This includes a clear expression of how important phone calls are (better than texting). Taking a few minutes several times a day to say hello is more important than you may realize. It sets a standard of availability that becomes part of a reassuring background.

If either you or your new partner allow absences to become a part of your relationship you run the risk that it becomes "habitual". Here's how that works. When one is absent the other feels a loss. If the person feeling the loss does not protest, the person who is absent starts to feel their love is not important. They may get angry or sad about this and thus they are absent more. The person feeling the loss may not protest because they don't feel they are worth the love that is not available. The longer they experience the loss the angrier or sadder they get and therefore are not about to confront the absent partner.

One of the most important ways to construct a "presence life" with someone new is to state clearly what you want and need, and why that feels good. For example, "I love it when you are with me. I seem to get more out of life" or, "I notice you've stopped calling as much. You should know that every time you call I get a warm feeling".

How Seniors Can Find Companionship or Marriage

You know that absence is sometimes unavoidable. But you should also know that your heart never thinks it leads to fondness.

TENDER WORDS

Direct from Your Heart

There's a good possibility that you have never referred to yourself as "honey", or "sweetie" or even "best ever".

These are words or descriptions that require two people – the one doing the labeling and you, the one being labeled. And since this type of verbal interaction has been happening in society for a long time, there must be a good reason for it. The reason is that it feels really nice when someone close talks tenderly to you.

Tender talk makes you feel special and good and valuable. It makes you want to stay and hear more.If you are in a new relationship, or desire to be in one, it is crucial that you master the art of tender talking. To help you here are some things to think about:

- Even though your relationship may be new, there are advantages to *using the tender words that you use or have used* with others.

What makes words really tender is the emotional tone that goes with them. Your use of certain words over years has given you a mastery of how effective they sound. If you have been calling those close to you "honey", then a switch to "sweetie" may sound hollow and won't get the desired results.

- The person you are starting with (or may soon start with) may have a *specific choice of what sounds tender* to them and request that you use it. In this case try it out and see if it can come natural to you.

HOW SENIORS CAN FIND COMPANIONSHIP OR MARRIAGE

There is more of a chance this will be successful if the response to you using this word is great enough to give you a lot of pleasure. "Love bunny" may seem hard to get out but if it leads to good sex you may get used to it.

- When you are first meeting a potential partner *use tender words sooner than later*. After all, if this new person is as eager to get into a relationship as you are, tender words will be experienced as a clear invitation. This is what could set you apart from others – your love is available and waiting to be claimed.

Your words tell a lot about you, but it is those tender words that tell about your heart. So use them well, Honey.

INFIDELITY

Insuring Faithfulness

Perhaps no other behavior causes such deep distress as infidelity. All the qualities that keep you in love – trust, dependability, availability, strength – these all seem lost when someone is unfaithful. If this has happened to you in a prior relationship you probably feel sensitized to it happening again with a new person. If it hasn't happened to you directly you know that it is not uncommon and that people are deeply hurt by it.

How best to avoid being cheated on in your new relationship? There are three things to do preventively:

> First understand what it's about. It's important to know that *unfaithful behavior is much more about the person who is doing the cheating* than the person being cheated on.

> It is usually about a life long difficulty with commitment and/or a pattern of testing an important person.

> Second, be aware of the *ways infidelity can be expressed*, especially early on in your relationship. It comes down to the simple question of whether you are being treated exclusively. So if your new person is talking intimately with other people when you are out socially, if they send or receive phone calls or text messages to former spouses or companions, if they continue to conduct unnecessary business with a former spouse – this is early infidelity.

How Seniors Can Find Companionship or Marriage

Third, know *what you can do to act upon infidelity* – with words and, possibly, action. The more direct and firm you are the better. There are two steps: *Identify what is happening* :"You're giving your time and attention to someone else" or, "I'm not feeling as exclusive with you as I'd like". After identifying *say what should happen*: "It would be better if you stopped texting the person you used to date" or, "When we're out socially I'd like you to concentrate more on me".

The success with which you handle infidelity early in your relationship will set the course for the rest of your life together. If your efforts fail then you have a difficult fact to face: that it would be better for you to start afresh with a new, and more faithful partner.

A faithful person like yourself deserves a faithful partner in a relationship.

GIVING GIFTS

And Receiving Them

You've started seeing someone on a regular basis. Since you both work, Friday and Saturday nights are when you go out. Shortly after you started seeing each other flowers began arriving every Saturday morning. It was a nice addition to what was already a promising relationship. The message seemed to be: "I'm enjoying our time together. Last night was great and I'm looking forward to tonight".

Then, recently, in addition to the flowers, your new person would bring something for you each time they came. Once it was a scarf, another time a modest piece of jewelry. These gifts seemed different than the flowers. In fact you probably never referred to the flowers as "gifts" at all.

As these gifts became a regular occurrence some questions started in your mind: Is our relationship entering a more serious phase? Are there some new expectations of me? Do they expect me to give gifts in return? These are questions more easily thought about than spoken.

So in new relationships are gifts a good thing?

In general, gifts should always be a good thing. They represent someone's good feelings toward you. They have to be chosen, purchased and sent – all implying that time and resources are involved.

There are some simple ways to understand and accept gifts so that they don't stir you up or result in discussions that may not be best for a new relationship.

HOW SENIORS CAN FIND COMPANIONSHIP OR MARRIAGE

- *Always acknowledge* gifts when you next see the person. This face to face thank you gives both of you the best way of enjoying the gift. "The earrings you sent are very attractive. As you see, I'm wearing them. You must have enjoyed picking them out". This interaction expresses gratitude, makes a statement about the value of the gift, and makes reference to the giver's competence in picking out something so nice.

A lot is accomplished between the two of you in relationship to the gift.

- If you think the gift is inappropriate to the beginning of a relationship – too personal or too expensive, *acknowledge but with a clear statement of your feelings*. "I'm sure you gave a lot of thought to your gift but since we're just getting to know each other, the time we spend together is enough of a gift for now".

This shows that you are capable of setting limits on the progression of the relationship while at the same time saying that it has value and possibility.

Gift giving will be a regular part of your new relationship. How you receive gifts can be impressive and endearing to your new partner. That will bring you the most valuable gift of all – a great love.

You Don't Have to Live Alone

SPECIAL DAYS

Reflecting Your New Life

Of course special days started with your birthday – and that remains a very special day for you. You now share it with others but it continues to have a very personal and special feel for you. As you have moved through life you have added a lot more special days to your calendar – anniversaries (of marriages, and of deaths), birthdays of parents and children, and those private special days when you remember meeting someone very important or when something very important happened to you. Not to mention Thanksgiving, Christmas, etc.

Now that you are about to begin a new phase of your life, with a new partner, what about those special days you carry with you from your past? And, just as important, what about the special days that belong to your partner?

As you spend more and more of your time together you will have experiences that have a high emotional content –your first kiss, the evening you first have dinner together, the night your partner first stays over at your house and when you first introduce them to your family.

Mark these dates down so you can reference them when you want. They are your "new" special days and part of your new relationship. Your partner will be glad that you remember them as that shows how important you think they are.

With regard to your "old" special days, you know from reading YOU DON'T HAVE TO LIVE ALONE that your new partner wants to feel exclusive with you.

HOW SENIORS CAN FIND COMPANIONSHIP OR MARRIAGE

Therefore you have to think carefully about which "old" special days you quietly forget about. They will be the ones that have no relevance to your new partner or which reference another person that you were formerly involved with.

As your new relationship grows you will be wise enough to construct a calendar of special days that is truly, and exclusively, a reflection of your new life together.

You Don't Have to Live Alone

HOLDING BACK

A Normal Part of Moving Ahead

When you sense that something exciting is about to happen your tendencies are twofold: to rush ahead and experience, but also to hold back and be cautious. The reason for the second tendency - to hold back- is because "exciting" often implies "new" and new carries some anxiety with it. This is a pattern you probably have experienced as you do all the things necessary to find a significant companion or spouse.

Here are some examples of holding back:

> You kept asking your friend at the weekly book club for the name of the new accountant in her office. She had described him as very nice and recently divorced. When she finally gave you his name and mentioned he was expecting your email you found that weeks went by before you contacted him.

> When you were with your friends at the bowling alley you sat next to a very talkative and attractive gal when you were having beers at the bar. She touched your arm several times as she talked and indicated she bowled there every Tuesday night. You didn't get her name but said you'd see her next Tuesday. Over the next month you found excuses not to go bowling even though you thought of her often.

In both of these examples (whichever one applics) you wanted to get into a new relationship but held back. The purpose of this discussion is not to eliminate holding back (although it might happen less) but rather to make your experience with it easier. Understanding that holding back may be serving an important function – to provide caution – may make you less hard on yourself when it happens. So don't jump to the conclusion that you didn't really want that person anyway, or that you are fundamentally flawed.

Holding back, in any of the ways it might occur, is a normal part of "new relationship" behavior. Some do it more than others depending on development and life's experiences. When it happens to you - understand it as much as possible, get past it as soon as possible, and, if necessary, explain it to your new partner as effectively as possible.

OVERCOMING MEMORIES

Do it Successfully

Good times or bad times, they all leave memories. These memories are in your head and you make them reappear when you want to relive something, or they may come forward on their own.

As a new relationship is about the future it can be helpful to understand how memories may complicate things. For example: You have just met someone and the friendship phase has gone quite well. Understandably you wonder when the first kiss will occur. When it does happen, as you are sitting in the local Mexican restaurant, you find yourself remembering the way your deceased spouse used to kiss. This memory may make you confused, or sad, or both.

This memory has come back at the worst possible moment. It makes it hard to feel passionate and causes you to hold back from exchanging another kiss. You may ask yourself if this is likely to happen again. Could it even jeopardize this new relationship?

Memories that arise during your new relationship are, by definition, from your past. However, their appearance does follow some general rules and knowing these rules will help overcome those memories that may cause trouble.

First, memories can come from emotional associations. As you were enjoying the Mexican dinner with your new partner the general emotion was of pleasure in being with a caring person. So when the kiss occurred it made sense that the memory that came forth was also associated with being with a caring person – your deceased spouse.

Second, memories are also called up by the occurrence of specific and similar circumstances. So if you spent many years eating at restaurants with your deceased spouse then being in a restaurant with this new partner makes the memory that came forth very predictable.

Memories that occur in your new relationship make sense. They follow rules and should not be interpreted as any kind of judgement about this new person. If a memory makes you uncomfortable, thinking about how it works will allow you to disregard or overcome it.

Of course it is important to note that there are also memories that are comfortable and that seem to support the feelings you are having with your new partner. Enjoy them as you would a good burrito.

BEGINNING TALK

Voice and Words Together

There is a lot of talk out there. When you meet a "person of interest" you want to make sure that your voice and the words it makes are unique. As that person listens to you talk you want them to be thinking, "I think something good and exciting is happening now".

As I'm sure you realize by now, when I talk to you in YOU DON'T HAVE TO LIVE ALONE I use my voice very carefully and pick words that will be helpful. So the words "good" and "exciting" are important. They represent what any potential partner will be looking for. "Good" represents your ability to give them care, and "exciting" represents the promise of positive things to come.

Your beginning talk can be effective by the *sound of your voice* and the *words that you choose.*

Your *voice sound* should be: *softer rather than loud* - if you are in a loud atmosphere, rather than keeping your voice loud, suggest to the new person that you move to a quieter spot or go outside. Tell them clearly that you will have a better conversation that way; *calmer rather than stirred up* - if you are describing a wild and crazy friend, talk clearly about your own more controlled way of living, and *constant* - in describing other people's emotional ups and downs keep your own voice at the same level.

Your *choice of words* should *represent your usual vocabulary* - if the new person seems to use slang or popular phrases don't try to adapt to or imitate their talk; stay who you are.

It will allow you to be more natural and the new person sees clearly what they're getting. Also, your speech should be *free of curse words* - if cursing is part of your usual vocabulary try to keep it out of these early conversations – cursing is angry talk and that's not the way you want to present yourself. Finally there should be lots of *support and connection words* - "I know exactly what you mean", "You have a lot of interesting ideas", "I've often felt that way", "I'd love to hear more".

The right combination of voice sound and words can be a powerful attractor as beginning talk becomes an ongoing relationship.

USING YOUR BODY

To Show You Care

There are many pebbles on the beach. When you pick one up the others fade into the background. The pebble in your hand is the one you pay attention to. You feel its surface, examine its color and patterns and become familiar with its weight and heft in your hand. You then decide whether to throw it out to sea or put it in your pocket and take it home.

When someone first feels the tug of attraction for you, their intent is to examine you more closely. As they get to know you through talk and activities, it is your body which sends out vital information about your ability to be a good partner. The signals you send have to do with *presence, touch,* and *receptiveness.*

Presence – This has to do with how available your body is and how it feels to the person of interest. An important measure of availability is closeness. Stand close, sit close; be right next to the person; let your bodies touch whenever possible. Arm around their waist, taking every opportunity to hug, wearing clothing that feels soft – all give a sense of body presence that feels good.

Touch – When you touch your partner you make a connection with them. It's a feeling bridge between your bodies. Touching is a re-minder of your body. Your partner is not going to fall in love with your hand when you touch them; they fall in love with where your hand extends from – your body. Take every possible opportunity to touch your special person; it can't be done too often. In fact, the more it's done, the more it's desired.

Receptiveness – Your new companion will need to test how you feel about them. An important way is through touching, the touching they extend to you. They want to feel that their touch is very powerful, that you welcome it and appreciate it. They only way they will know is by your receptiveness to it. They want to see that you don't pull away, that you reciprocate and, perhaps, speak about how it feels good. If they lean into you they want you to lean back. If they initiate a hug they'll want you to melt into them.

Using your body properly will surely get you into that special person's pocket – like the pebble, they'll take you home and keep you forever.

ALL ABOUT ALCOHOL

Make it Work for You

To put it simply, alcohol can change everything. Big change, small change; change you notice, change that goes unnoticed; change that makes things seem better, change that definitely makes things worse. As alcohol affects your senses, your emotions and the way you process the world, it has the ability to change a lot.

Searching for a significant companion or spouse may put you in a variety of situations where you use alcohol yourself or associate with others who use it. I am assuming that through a lot of experience you have learned how to handle alcohol appropriately. You know what forms of alcohol have desirable effects and which can make you uncomfortable.

Here are some things to consider about alcohol use that can be helpful in your search:

> - If someone has made a positive impression on you, and there was alcohol use by either you or the other person, arrange to have a social interaction that is alcohol-free. Then confirm your impression without the alcohol effect present. Alcohol lowers inhibitions, thereby leading to an easy manner and conversation. Although this may feel positive in the moment, you want an ongoing relationship to become comfortable based on how you experience each other substance-free.

- If your prospective partner insists on socializing, in public or private, with alcohol in use – beware! It might indicate that alcohol is an issue for them and that they don't feel able to socialize without it.

- If you are about to engage in a new social situation with someone who you have positive expectations of - you may have had encouraging communication by phone or online, or they may come highly recommended by friends - feel free to take advantage of the anxiety-reducing effects of alcohol. It may not be the true "substance-free you" but it could get you feeling more confident and attractive. This, in turn, gets you farther along in the relationship than you were before. This is a smart and limited use of alcohol.

Let's toast your new relationship!

STRONG AS A MAGNET

Will be Very Attracting

You are very aware of the time and energy you spend looking for the right companion. What is equally important is the time and energy that someone is spending looking for you. What about you is most likely to attract someone? Even the word "attract" is perfectly descriptive of what goes on. It implies that somebody will be drawn toward you, that the closer they get, the greater the pull.

The quality that will draw that special someone toward you, like an iron filing to a magnet, is your strength. Of all the qualities that you possess, the one that promises the most secure and happy future is your ability to be strong. If you show it early and often your ability to attract a special person will be great. You just need to point the magnet – your strength – in the direction of the one you choose.

Your opportunities to show your strength are many; the especially important ones have to do with initial attraction and establishing the routine of a relationship.

Initial attraction – This would include first contacts: "Hi, I've been watching you and listening to you talk. It would be good to get to know each other" – There is no doubt in this statement, no question, just a clear statement of interest and intent. Or, "We exchanged information last week but you haven't called. I would like to get to know you better. Please call me sooner rather than later") - This is a clear statement of interest with an expectation attached. These examples set up clear guidelines for getting to know a person of interest. They show that you are strong, and the person who experiences that will be positively attracted.

How Seniors Can Find Companionship or Marriage

Routine of a relationship – Routines can be very reassuring, and if you are part of those routines that increases your attractiveness.

Being strong in encouraging and maintaining those routines will be welcomed by your new partner. "I love that Italian restaurant you took me to. Let's go there again". This is a clear message about a nice experience shared together. It also strongly suggests repeating it. Or, "I love when you call me at lunchtime. I'm glad I can look forward to it every day". Again, you strongly take a nice experience for you both and make it something to be repeated.

Properly and strongly magnetized, you will "never be alone".

HOW YOU THINK

Avoiding Negative Patterns

Thinking about meeting someone and becoming involved in a relationship may seem confusing at times. It can help to know about some basic thinking patterns that can occur in this kind of situation. These patterns are very common but that doesn't make them any less difficult. They occur as two basic types: the *I'll never meet anyone* type and the *this will never last* type. Both types are characterized by a desire to protect yourself and neither type is necessarily what you truly believe. Let's try to give you a better understanding of them:

> *I'll never meet anyone* – When you want something very much and have tried long and hard to get it a type of deprivation feeling sets in. Feeling deprived makes you tend to think about the thing you want a lot.

> Telling yourself you'll never get it reduces the pressure to keep looking; it also reduces the pain of not having. It's an attempt to adapt to your present single state. This of course is something that you don't want to do.

> *This will never last* – When you finally get what you've wanted – a good relationship which will provide companionship and perhaps marriage – the good feelings may actually be hard to accept. They may feel so good that the idea of losing them can be very difficult. It would be protective to think they won't last, but also very sad, and not a good way to proceed forward.

If you find yourself involved in either of these patterns of thinking – try to step back from the situation and use your understanding of how they work. The good news is that having these thoughts indicates that you truly want a great relationship – or have found it.

ON THE REBOUND

Catch and Keep

When you catch a ball on the rebound you assume it's the same ball you threw (or hit) away from you. You also assume that it is able to continue bouncing its usual way when you throw (or hit) it away from you once again. There is nothing wrong with the ball because it rebounded to you – it's still your trusty ball.

In your game of romance, the game of finding the right partner, being "on the rebound" may have some negative connotations that we want to get rid of. Let's talk about what a rebound is and how to turn it to your advantage.

The negative connotations of being on the rebound have to do with the fact that your new potential relationship is somehow compromised by a past relationship.

There is also the implication your new person is hurting in some way because of their breakup experience.

In fact, even if all of that is true there are opportunities for you to take advantage of. A person coming from a failed relationship will be in a good position to appreciate your good care by comparison. They will also have had time to know what they are looking for.

When you begin a relationship with this "rebounded" person remember that they would like to be hopeful about you rather than dwell on who they used to be with. If they start talking about the old relationship say something like, "That was then; this is now. It would be best to talk about us".

HOW SENIORS CAN FIND COMPANIONSHIP OR MARRIAGE

The more you can keep things in the present, being optimistic about your future together, the sooner you will have the rebound issue behind you both.

YOUR FRIENDS

Changes Will Occur

During your unattached years you have probably collected a number of people, some that you see singly, others that you see in a group. This is your circle of friends. They have filled empty hours and given you people to talk to when you needed to talk. Now that you are seriously looking to be in a significant relationship, these friends have to be considered.

Are they a help or a hindrance? Do they serve as a source of encouraging support or do they regard you as necessary to the group, not to be lost. You may find that they will be eager to hear about the new person you've met. You may also find that, over time, their initial interest turns either to disinterest or to looking for fault.

When you bring this important person to events where your friends are present there may be some inappropriate behavior on their part– either outright hostility or instances of competitive closeness.

As time goes by, and you find this new relationship progressing there may be some uneasiness in your mind about spending more time with your new person and less time with your friends. This is both inevitable and desirable. You only have a certain amount of time and energy and you want it to be spent in the way that's best for you. A good message to your friends could be, "I know you are happy that I've found someone I care about. When I am not with you I think how important you've been to me."

Once your time is taken more and more with your new person, something else may occur – your friends may stop calling as frequently as they used to, or they may make plans without including you. This may be troubling to you, but it makes sense to them. Hearing about your new relationship may stir them up - "why can't I find someone?" or, "I'll never find someone as nice" or, "She doesn't deserve him".

Whatever your friends' behavior, you'll do best by trying to hold onto the most supportive of them as you proceed with your partner. You can say something like, "I have two hearts – one for you and one for Dave". Of course you and I know that the bigger heart belongs to Dave.

SING A SONG

You'll Both be Happy

When you start to have contact with a prospective partner it's important to send signals that it would be desirable to spend time with you. In YOU DON'T HAVE TO LIVE ALONE I have talked about some significant ways to send these signals – through your communications, by your reactions, and with your body. This next signal could be the one that closes the deal.

When is the last time you heard someone singing in the shower, including yourself? It is the one vocalization that is universally associated with being happy. The shower is not the important part. The important part is that you are by yourself in the shower, and if you sing by yourself you must really be happy. Singing by or to yourself is something you've done since you were very young. So has your companion, and so they know the good things that it represents.

There can be many opportunities to do this singing when the special person is around. I've already mentioned the shower. However you can sing along with a song you hear on the radio or your IPod. You can sing when you cook, when you do a craft, etc. Words aren't even necessary; humming a tune is also effective.

If your new companion comments on your singing, let them know that you do it because you feel good inside. Don't be surprised if they start singing or humming more themselves.

Singing represents happiness; happiness is contagious and is a great romantic facilitator.

SOMEONE LIKE YOU

Yours for the Making

You've done a lot of living. You know what you like for breakfast, you know how many hours of sleep you need, you know where you like to sit at the movies. Certain routines and activities are tried and true. How do you maintain your comfortable life if you meet someone and fall in love with them? They will have their own likes and dislikes, their own way of living, their own pet peeves. Yes, you'll want to be with them, but will being with them cause more discomfort than the relationship is worth? How can you meet someone like you?

This would seem to be a major issue for you, simply because of your age and stage in life. Happily it does not have to be. There are two reasons why you can meet a significant someone and form a living style together that makes you both happy.

The first reason is that many of your life routines and preferences may come from earlier relationships and have continued by habit. If you are divorced or your spouse has passed away there were many things that were done for so long together that you don't actually think about giving them up or changing them. If you always sat in the first few rows of the theater that may seem like the natural spot to watch movies. If you had grapefruit juice every morning that has also become one of your automatic choices.

So now that you are entering a new relationship the everyday things you do together can seem exciting and refreshing. Imagine, seeing a movie from the middle of the theater and enjoying the taste of grape juice for breakfast.

How Seniors Can Find Companionship or Marriage

The second reason to be optimistic about liking the same things and enjoying the same routines with a new person is your desire to accommodate based on feelings of love.

When you are feeling secure with your new person it is easy to be adventuresome. You may never have had the slightest desire to eat sushi, but when your new partner wants to try it you are all too happy to try raw fish. You always considered 3D movies for kids but when a new 3D movie gets great reviews the two of you are willing to give it a try – because you'll be in a new experience together.

So finding someone like you happens naturally – because it gives you an opportunity to break with some of your past and allows both of you the excitement of a new future together.

SURPRISES

The Good and Bad

Surprises keep life interesting. As much as we try to create and maintain routine and security there have to be surprises as well. A new relationship will offer you many surprises – it's up to you to enjoy them or deal with them in an effective way.

If you are just getting to know a new special person there will be many *initial surprises*: what they look like, how they treat you, what they like to eat, how they interact physically with you, and many more. These surprises are relatively easy to handle. They are expectable since they are about newness. They are also easy because they occur when you are feeling hopeful about this new situation.

As your relationship proceeds there may be other *ongoing surprises* which are more challenging.

These have to do with your new person's personal circumstances - grown children who may suddenly call and require time and assistance, a job requirement that conflicts with your time together, the appearance of a messy ointment that helps arthritis pain, the need to bite fingernails, etc. These surprises are not expectable and may seem to suggest a problem for the long term. I suggest that when they arise you be direct about paying attention to them and addressing them when necessary as time goes by.

With these types of surprises you want to feel that somehow they make sense and that you will be able to adapt to them or work with your partner to change them.

So far I have talked about surprises that happen to you. There is also the benefit of surprises that you make happen; these can positively affect your new relationship.

Examples are: sending the special person an e-card with a special message, wearing a new perfume, making a meal that they talked about liking, arranging for a weekend away together, etc. When you are in charge of the surprises you avoid the discomfort and enjoy the pleasure.

Whatever way surprises occur in your relationship, the biggest and nicest surprise will be the way you make it work for you.

GETTING ATTENTION

All You Want

When you are in the process of finding someone new and starting a relationship with them, you will still have needs, just like you usually do. There may be mornings when you get up with a backache. You may be in a period where your hemorrhoids are acting up. Your new glasses may be causing a headache. Your weight may be causing you to watch what you eat.

How you deal with these types of discomfort when you are still in that special beginning phase of a relationship will be important – it is a time you want to appear attractive, a time you want your new person to start thinking of you as a forever companion. You may need some attention, but don't want to be a "complainer".

I know it may seem like a tricky balance – getting the attention you need and making your new person feel good about giving it to you. The trick is to appear strong as you ask for the attention and making your person feel strong as they respond to you.

Here are things you might say about the need situations I mentioned above: Backache - "Let's have a nice relaxing evening at my place. I love watching movies with you"; Hemorrhoids - "If I spend some extra time in the bathroom I know you have the common sense not to ask why"; Headache - "These new glasses take some getting used to. Do you have any ideas about adjusting the frames?"; Weight watching - "I've been eating too heavily lately. Why don't you pick a nice place for a light bite".

Using the right words will get the attention of your companion in the best way - and your companion will then shower attention on you.

How Seniors Can Find Companionship or Marriage

BEING HONEST

Consider the Feelings

The issue of honesty involves two people – the one who is being "honest", and the one who receives the "honest" words. The purpose of being honest is to instill trust in a relationship. Trust implies that good care is and will be available.

When you meet a person of interest, you want to attract them to you, and then keep them with you. This is most likely to happen when they can be sure of good care from you, when they trust that you will always give them good care. Therefore it seems logical than you should be honest with them.

In fact, as important as honesty is, it is the "best policy" in a relationship only when used wisely. This is because you can be honest with your companion, but miss what is happening emotionally at the same time.

For example, the new person you've met is seriously balding and is obviously bothered by it. You see that they've fixed their hair to make the most of what is left and they often touch their hair self consciously. One night, at dinner, the question comes up, "Sometimes going bald really bothers me. What do you think of my hair?"

It would be simple to be honest and say "Oh, I love your hair just the way it is". But you can do better than that. You can be honest with what is happening emotionally and have much greater impact. You could say, "I'm glad you feel comfortable enough to bring up your baldness. I can tell it's really something you think about. If you can get comfortable going bald so can I".

How Seniors Can Find Companionship or Marriage

Just as I try to do in YOU DON'T HAVE TO LIVE ALONE, let your honest words go beyond the facts; get to the feelings that are there as well.

MATURE LOVE

A Definite Advantage

Is falling in love now different than when you were younger? The answer is yes, and no. Does being more mature mean that you will handle a relationship better now than you would have in the past? The answer is yes, and no. Maturity does bring experience but experience does not necessarily insure success.

The best way to make your maturity an advantage is to use your experience, while also being in love the way you always have been. Think of it this way –you both should have an older mind and a younger heart.

Consider your search situation. You've made some contacts, talked to several available people on the phone and had a few dinners. So far the right person hasn't surfaced.

Tonight you have a coffee date with someone who sounded promising on the phone. Your past experience has made you apprehensive about this meeting. You are questioning the likelihood of this person working out. And yet, you are still excited about the possibilities. Is this confusing? Are you fooling yourself? Setting yourself up for disappointment?

What's happening is the maturity of experience along with the hope of young love. It is mature love and you make it work for you by understanding it. Your experience lets you know there can be no guarantee at this point, but your young heart still enjoys fantasizing about what might happen – all this allows you to make the most of this date tonight. You will show your romantic self while being able to evaluate this new person realistically.

HOW SENIORS CAN FIND COMPANIONSHIP OR MARRIAGE

Your mature love can make you very attractive – experienced and romantic at the same time.

WIDOW OR WIDOWER

Moving Forward

If your search for a partner leads you to someone who has lost a spouse through death the feelings you have could be complicated. On one hand they have become available to you because they have lost a partner themselves. On the other hand their loss has given you an opportunity for companionship. On one hand you would expect them to have some sadness about their loss and on the other hand you will be trying to make a relationship with them filled with happiness.

An important question for you to ask the new person right away is how long it has been since they lost their spouse. This question is factually important to you because it is not a good idea to start a relationship too soon after the death. Too soon generally means less than six months.

If you find out that it is too soon you might say, "I think it will be fairest for both of us to wait a little longer. Let's pick a date a few months from now and put it on our calendars. That's when we can get together again".

Once you have started to see each other it's important to be respectful of both the deceased spouse and your relationship. Your new partner may bring up the deceased spouse in conversation, remembering what they did together or subtly comparing them with you. You may hear something like, "We loved going to the beach together" or, "Her lasagna tasted a lot like yours".

How Seniors Can Find Companionship or Marriage

A good rule to follow is for you not to bring up the deceased spouse in your conversations. This allows for a clean and new relationship to develop between you. It is the best emotionally as sadness is not stirred up.

If you find your new companion is frequently referencing their deceased spouse you might say something like, "I know they were very important to you but you'll feel best if you focus on us". This is doing them a favor as they can move into your new relationship with a minimum of sadness or looking back.

Marrying a widow or widower can be an advantage to you as there are a minimum of strings attached. Any strings that do remain you will gently cut.

FIRST IMPRESSIONS

Only a Beginning

You've heard what they say about first impressions – that you shouldn't go by them, that they can be deceiving, that you need more time to really get to know someone. You know all of this is true. You've been meeting people and forming opinions for many years. What is also true is that when you want very much to meet a special person the first impression can seem very important. This may be the basis for further contact or a decision to try someone else.

When you really want a relationship, the first contact can make you either overly receptive or overly critical. Presumably the other person is experiencing the same things.

There is not only the effort to make a judgment, but also to make an impression at the same time. You want to look good and to seem interesting. That's a lot going on for what might be a limited period of time. If you get the chance you might even say something like, "I'm sure we both realize how first impressions seem both important and difficult".

My suggestion is that you take the first impression as a *general* measure. If you feel generally positive - more positive than negative - about the new person then further time together is probably wise. It shows that you both passed the first test, despite all the emotions and uncertainties that were present.

How Seniors Can Find Companionship or Marriage

All your subsequent meetings with each other will occur knowing what you both look like and how you both sound. This is basic background information and will make further impressions easier to process.

If all goes well, your first impressions will be replaced by many good impressions.

MY BEST FRIEND

A Real Comfort

As you have moved through your life you have been both lucky and unlucky with the friends you've made. Circumstances like where you worked, who lived nearby, and with whom your partner or companions enjoyed socializing played a big part in your social time. As a result you now have pretty strict guidelines in your mind about the qualities you look for in a friend.

If you have limitations like physical disabilities or financial worries, your guidelines for friendship are even more firm. Why would you enjoy the company of someone who wants to be out socializing when you would prefer quiet time at home? Why would you put up with someone whose ideas about spending money were very different than your own? How could you enjoy physically demanding activities when you have trouble walking?

These questions about the appropriateness of with whom you spend time mean that your search for a companion will feel successful when you find someone who meets your needs without making you uncomfortable.

"Staying put", sitting together, talking quietly and sharing memories can be restful and reassuring when you spend time with someone who enjoys your company as much as you enjoy theirs.

Just as circumstances influenced your earlier friendships, your life today may provide the opportunities for comfort and companionship. It may be the person you met at the doctor's office or the home companion provided for you by your social worker.

HOW SENIORS CAN FIND COMPANIONSHIP OR MARRIAGE

Whoever it is, wherever you meet them, you will have a "best friend" in the ways that are important at this time in your life.

GETTING COMMITTED

Love Forever

What's the difference between being forty-seven years old or seventy-four years old? The differences may have to do with the number of wrinkles, how much energy is present and when is bedtime. Where there is no difference is in the mind. Both age minds are of the moment, and both age minds believe they will exist forever.

This amazing quality of the mind is why I wrote YOU DON'T HAVE TO LIVE ALONE. Essentially everyone who is looking for a partner wants love now and wants it forever. You want a successful search resulting in a forever commitment.

All your efforts to meet someone, communicate, and spend time with them have been for the purpose of having them commit to you.

It's important to know that it will never be just you thinking about being committed. Therefore, if the person you have been seeing is not mentioning being with you forever you should not hesitate to mention it yourself. Don't put it in terms of a question, but rather a statement. Such a statement might be, "What we have feels so good I know we both want it to go on forever".

The issue of what form "forever" takes may cause some significant discussions. One of you may feel marriage is the only true commitment while the other has practical or circumstantial objections to that idea.

What is most important, marriage or not, is a mutual way of describing your relationship, to yourselves, and to others.

If you decide to marry, "Mr. and Mrs." has that official ring. But if you don't get joined formally you could call yourselves "permanent partners" or "companions forever." The label should be used repeatedly so that over time it has a forever feel to it. It is the forever feel that will help bond you together.

To sum it all up – Find love as soon as possible and keep it forever.

YOU DON'T HAVE TO LIVE ALONE

SPECIAL CARE SECTION

In this Special Care Section of **YOU DON'T HAVE TO LIVE ALONE** you will find a number of ways to feel that people can **care about you**, that people can **do for you**, and that people are **there for you**. In other words, even though you may be unattached or live alone, you never have to feel that you are alone.

There are many more people available than you may have realized. Whether it is **mealtime, relaxing time, bedtime or social time** – you can have someone who knows what you need and can tell you how to get it. Whether it is about your **health, medications or health care providers** – there are ways to get what is necessary so you can live a healthy life. Whether it involves **getting out and about or having others visit** – you can find those who want to share your company or will make sure you don't stay isolated at home. Whether it involves **learning new skills yourself or relying on experts** – you can find instruction or assistance you can trust.

On the following pages you can find what you need to **YOU DON'T HAVE TO LIVE ALONE**. I've listed the **Issues** that are of interest to you. Under each of the Issue headings you will find organizations, agencies or individuals that are available. You can then call or use them by using the **Contact Information** that I have provided. In addition to the actual Contact Information there are descriptions of why and how they might be useful. **Read on for the care you deserve**!

Special Care – Food and Eating

Eating meals should be one of your greatest pleasures. However, when you are by yourself there can be issues about choice, availability or safety of the food you eat.

Nutrition.gov – is where you can find information on healthy eating, dietary supplements, special senior nutrition, food safety, food shopping, cooking, meal planning and weight management. There is also information about an elderly nutrition assistance program, including home delivery.

FNIC - is the food and nutrition information center. Call **301-504-5414** and talk to a nutrition information specialist. Make your nutrition as good as it can be.

Food stamps –If you think they would be helpful, get eligibility and facts from the people at **800-772-1213**.

Food/drug or medication interactions – Visit **FamilyDoctor.org**. - Better to know than to worry.

Food shopping and delivery –– The folks at your city or state **Department of Social Services** can suggest services that may be useful.

Eating out – An inexpensive and supportive place to eat is at your nearby **Senior Center**.

(The Socialization section tells you how to locate Senior Centers). Also, local restaurant associations may offer **discount dining coupons**. Inquire about this at your local **Chamber of Commerce**.

Special Care – Safety and Mobility

When you live by yourself it is especially important that you be able to get around and get around safely. As you read through this section you will see that others are concerned about you and are available to you.

You Don't Have to Live Alone

<u>**Homemaker assistance and transportation**</u> – Really good information from **AoA** –the **Administration on Aging**. Visit **aoa.gov** or call **877-696-6775**.

<u>**Walker or wheelchair**</u>– You can get information, eligibility and sources from **Medicare**. Call **800-633-4227**.

<u>**Safety information**</u> – Being smart and prepared can make you feel more secure and able to handle some unforeseen incident. Good resources are: **Emergencycareforyou.org** –for safety tips, avoiding falls, travel to the doctor and injury protection. **Homesafetycouncil.org** – provides tips to prevent falls, safety checklists for your kitchen, garage, bathroom or basement.

As walking is a very beneficial activity you want to do it as safely as possible – visit the folks at **sparkpeople.com/fitness/resources** for useful tips. Also **familydoctor.org** offers safe exercise routines. The professionals at your local **hospital emergency room** should have brochures about avoiding accidents as well.

Concerning your basic systems like power or water – you do have some backup and guidance through your local **Power or Water company**. They publish safety guidelines and have outreach consultants available to you.

Knowing you have good protective backup is important to you also. **Consumerreports.org** helps you to learn about and compare alarms, sensors, detectors and alert buttons. Be sure to learn about elderly response programs that may be offered by your local **police and fire departments**.

Special Care – Medical Needs

When you get sick or have to contend with illness, being on your own can create additional stress or anxiety. The following resources should help.

AARP – An organization dedicated to the wellbeing of seniors. Even if you are not a member many of their information sources are available. Visit **aarp.org**.

Basic medical care-Whether or not you are 65 years of age, you should be familiar with the **Medicare** system. To learn about benefits, eligibility and participating doctors call **800-772-1213** or visit **socialsecurity.gov**. You can also visit **Healthcare.gov** or call **800-633-4227** to learn about insurance options, prevention and the Medicare system.

Eldercare - This general term refers to a broad group of services that meets the needs of seniors. These services often consist of in-home care and health insurance. To find eldercare services that may be appropriate for you contact - **AoA Eldercare locator** at **800-677-1116**.

Visiting Nurses – This organization provides home care visits, education programs and medical-related products. Find out more about **VNAA**, The Visiting Nurses Association and chapters that are near you. Call **202-384-1444**.

Drug pricing and comparison – If you feel confused about your medication, or the larger subject of medicine effectiveness or cost – All major pharmacy chains as well as Walmart, Target, etc. have drug pricing, generic information, safety and interactions available through the pharmacist on call or through their websites.

Special Care – Sleep and Bedtime

One of the most personal areas of your life is sleep and the bedtime and nighttime circumstances that are part of it. It is especially important that you feel secure and that you create an atmosphere of comfort around your sleep.

Sleep habits - For a good discussion of healthy sleep habits for seniors, including issues of disturbed sleep, insomnia, waking up tired and the effects of medica-

YOU DON'T HAVE TO LIVE ALONE

tion – visit **HELPGUIDE.org**. To read about frequently asked questions relating to sleep and aging – visit **healthfinder.gov**. Also, **SAFESENIORS.org** has good tips for restful sleep as well as the effects of lost sleep.

When you visit **your doctor** it is an opportunity to mention and discuss any persistent sleep problems.

General sleep issues - Knowing factors capable of affecting your sleep is important. These include bedtime habits, alcohol, reading and bathing.

Also talk to friends or family members about their ideas for good sleep – making a good bed selection, the use of a nightlight and safe furniture arrangement.

It is also reassuring to have a few people you trust who are willing to take a call from you in the middle of the night.

Special Care – Social and Community

Socialization can improve your health and your general quality of life. It keeps your mental abilities sharp and keeps you feeling valuable and important.

Senior Centers – These are very valuable to you. They have programs that improve health, enhance economic security and promote independence and dignity. To find senior centers in your community – **Mealall.org** is a website that has a convenient list of states that each list all their senior centers. These centers can help you find support in your community for chronic diseases like diabetes. They sponsor health workshops; they have programs that deliver meals to you regularly or occasionally, or sponsor congregate meals; they have links to, or sponsor, assisted living by helping with home care visitors.

Eldercare – These services are excellent when families or friends are not available. They provide opportunities to talk, share, and laugh. Practical help may include help with your hair, cooking, doctor visits, cleaning, walks, help with your computer or help with simple finances. Go to **eldercare.gov** to find the eldercare locator, or call **800-677-1116**. This is a service of the Administration on Aging (A0A). There are also community based eldercare services. Locate these through **Senior Centers** or through state or municipal **Departments of Social Service**.

<u>**Community Resources**</u> - **Schools** often have programs – volunteers who will visit you and socialize. Call your local **School Board** to find out about them. **Churches** also have social and supportive **Outreach** programs. Call your community houses of worship and talk to the **minister, pastor, priest or rabbi**. Socialize through **exercise** – groups or classes are offered by **Senior Centers, Eldercare facilities** or private **fitness centers**. Other enjoyable social activities include **bingo, cooking classes** and **dancing**. Check with your local **Chamber of Commerce** to get names and phone numbers of appropriate organizations. Also inquire at local **churches**.

Look at your **local newspapers** (especially the free ones) to find activities that appeal to you.

Special Care – Legal Issues and Protecting Yourself

When you are by yourself, a major area of insecurity or vulnerability is how to know about, and use, the law and the protective legal system. The following should help.

<u>General Security</u> – For general security always keep your cellphone nearby, with **911** on automatic dial. Find out about **neighborhood crime watch** programs from your **local police department**. The **police** in your **local precinct** can also tell you about **Outreach programs** they sponsor. Also, the **NCEA – National Center on Elder Abuse** - visit **ncea.aoa.gov** to find state laws specific to your location.

Scams, Fraud and Protecting your finances – Offices of the **State Attorney General** have special contacts and resources for seniors. You can report suspected fraud to them. Also, **LawForSeniors.org** –This organization deals with consumer scams; debt, divorce and remarriage issues; losing a spouse, pension issues and social security income.

In addition **nsclc.org** – the **National Senior Citizens Law Center** – protects the rights of low income seniors. Call them at **202-289-6976**.

In conclusion, be assured that all of the above resources exist to make your everyday living more secure and worry-free. Use these people and organizations when you need to, and you will **YOU DON'T HAVE TO LIVE ALONE.**

Dr. Carl Metzger

YOU DON'T HAVE TO LIVE ALONE

OPPORTUNITY AND RESOURCE SECTION

<u>Where to Begin</u>

The internet has essentially replaced the phone book. Every organization has a website. You don't even have to look through the yellow pages - you save time and energy searching for, and reading through, web sites. All you have to do is Google your topic!

Am I going too fast? If you are internet savvy, skip the rest of this section and dive right in to some great suggestions of where to make great social connections using the internet as your primary source of phone numbers, and dates and times of activities. If you are a little intimidated by the World Wide Web (i.e. The Internet), your best source of help is at your local library. Not only can the librarians help you learn to use the web, most libraries have computers available for you to use. No need to buy anything! And if you don't want help from a librarian, try your niece, your grandson, a neighbor -someone near you is bound to be internet savvy!

Can't get to the library? Phone them and ask them to search for, and give you information about, the organizations that are of interest to you.

But get there if you can. If you really don't want to get involved with using the computers yourself, have the librarian search for you - get the information you want about local Senior Centers and the programs they offer. Get information about Church Groups, Alumni Reunions, and Volunteer Opportunities. As you watch the librarian, you'll probably see how easy it is to use a search engine such as Google to type in the kind of information you are looking for, and to see what

How Seniors Can Find Companionship or Marriage

results you get. Also have the librarian show you how to find a particular site - you can search by the name of the organization (such as 'AARP'), or by going directly to the site if you know the web address. Have the librarian show you how to navigate through the website - how to use the menus, how to recognize some basic properties of the site (is it a U.S. Government site with a ".gov" extension?). Have the librarian help you create a free email account (many sites offer this!) and how to use it. Now you have become familiar with the web and are ready to strike out into the great social world it presents. Consider the following: when you find a web site, the first page you see will be their display window to the world. Is this someplace you want to enter? Does their presentation appeal to you? What is your first impression?

An organization's web site should give you a summary of who they are and what they do. It should have well-labeled menu items that are easy to understand. You should be able to quickly determine if it is worth your time and energy to investigate further. Some sites have great names, but do not actually do what the name suggests. Some are snazzy and want you to pay money to join. Some are sparse, but give you a great deal of information.

Read carefully. If you are unsure, a good website will have a contact phone number. Use it! Find out all you can.

For various 'computer lessons' on everything from email etiquette to using various computer programs, try this site (you do not need to join):
www.gcflearnfree.org

Being Smart and Careful

One of the best ways to use the internet is to cross-check sites you find (searching for an independent review of a website you'd like to join). Let's say you find a terrific offer on a Cruise for Single Seniors on site X offered by cruise company Y. Use a search engine (such as Google or Yahoo) to search for "X Y recommendation". See if an independent site offers a review or testimony about the website and/or the cruise itself. So many sites offer ways to provide feedback that you should be able to learn more whether a site is trustworthy, whether an offer is genuine, what is really involved, and whether it is the right fit for you. And be sensitive to the information you give out about yourself on the web. A great source of safety rules for using the internet can be found on the NJ State Police site: **http://www.state.nj.us/njsp/tech/safe-teens.html**

Also, **Google "federal trade commission, consumer protection"** – to learn about privacy policies, avoiding scams, etc. If you make or respond to online or newspaper dating/friendship ads, keep in mind the following:

"DON'TS" FOR BOTH
NEWSPAPER ADS AND ONLINE –

Don't give out phone number or address until you get to know the person. If you start with e-mail – do it for a month before starting phone calls. On the first call use the phone company's I.D. blocker number (ask your phone company how to do this). For a first meeting – pick a public place, during daylight hours. Tell two or three friends when and where your meeting will be. After the first meeting don't go directly home – run some errands first.

You are smart, savvy, and strong - you didn't get this far without life skills. If you sense something isn't right, don't use that website, don't meet that person. Trust your gut. If something sounds too good to be true, it probably is.

Real people, good programs, excellent opportunities, all are worth taking the time to get to know, don't let yourself get rushed into anything. There are a lot of wonderful connections out there waiting for you - and you will find them!

HOW SENIORS CAN FIND COMPANIONSHIP OR MARRIAGE

General computer information - These sites give you a great start!

www.seniornet.org – for 50 plus computer users

www.seniorwomen.com – for senior women on the web

www.eons.com/cranky/ - an age-relevant search engine for social issues, games, etc.

www.aarp.org/onlinecommunity – for social networking (the site is a little cluttered, but offers many possibilities)

Senior groups – It's nice to have company.

www.aarp.org – the website for AARP – an umbrella and advocacy group for seniors.

www.linkdiscovery.com – provides senior sites, and groups, by city and state.

www.seniormeetup.com – for shared activities and interests, local chapters.

www.usa.gov/Topics/Seniors.shtml – for senior citizen resources.

www.theseniorlist.com – community based consumer reviews for seniors

Google "senior centers" – for centers in your community - fabulous opportunities!

Google "senior networking" – for appropriate social sites.

Google "(your city) government site" – search for "senior organizations".

Google "(your state) government site" – search for "senior organizations".

Google "Jewish Community Center" (your city) – search for activities, programs, etc.

Google YMCA (your city) – for programs, social occasions, groups, etc.

You Don't Have to Live Alone

<u>Social/Dating</u> - A world of possibilities –

IMPORTANT INFORMATION ABOUT INTERNET DATING AND PERSONAL NEWSPAPER ADS:

About Online & Newspaper Ads – The best personal ads feature privacy protection such as offering a phone number to hear a message recorded by you, the seeker. The reader can leave a responding phone message. These ad services cost on the basis of per minute phone time – so pay attention to how many calls you are making. Other ads protect your privacy by allowing you to use an email address or an ad 'online post box'. There may by charges associated with these as well - read the fine print!

Although there are very few newsprint personal sections in large urban papers now, you will find people much closer to you - and better ad prices - using your local community's publications. In addition to home delivery papers, some communities offer free publications available at every grocery store. Almost all have websites in addition to their print versions so your ad is seen by newspaper readers and internet users!

The free urban hip publications (such as The Eastbay Express and the Dallas Observer) feature some ads that offer rather explicit services. Be sure you find an online social site or newspaper that offers ads that match your sensibilities and what you yourself are looking for. There are many possibilities. Ads on one site (in one paper) may cater only to people in their 20's. Some to only pet lovers. Some make it easier to choose 'friendship' rather than 'romance'. If ads on one site seem too 'naughty', find another that features 'nice' ads. Some have both (those that let you choose 'naughty or nice' seem to get more traffic from seniors than those that make no distinction)!

HOW SENIORS CAN FIND COMPANIONSHIP OR MARRIAGE

Be sure to check each site's (or newspaper's) privacy policies with regard to phone number, address, etc. Some services are free. Those that charge usually offer a free introductory period (if you are asked to give a credit card for a free introductory period, be sure to set a reminder to check the date the free period expires!).

When composing an ad, be sure to mention the kind of person you are looking for – mention activities you like and would like to share. Mention personal qualities also – sense of humor, spontaneous, independent, etc. Most online ads allow photos. Find a flattering one of yourself that is a little generic (so your privacy is protected), but does reflect your age and personality.

If space is a premium, use these standard personal ad abbreviations (see below) to save space so you have room to add your personal descriptions.

Standard Personal Ad Abbreviations –

M – male
F – female
D – divorced
S – single
WW – widowed
W – white
A – Asian
J – Jewish
G – Gay
n/s – non-smoker
n/drugs – drug-free
LTR – long term relationship
h/w – height, weight

YOU DON'T HAVE TO LIVE ALONE

H – Hispanic

B – Black

NA – Native American

C – Christian

ISO – in search of

n/d – non-drinker

P – Professional

TLC – tender loving care

Dating/Social Websites –

www.seniorliving.about.com – good overview article.

www.freedating-sites.com/seniors.htm/ - describes types of social/ dating sites

www.aarp.org – search "dating sites and services".

www.theinternetdatingguide.com – references to multiple sites.

www.seniorpeoplemeet.com – meet, chat.

www.overfifties.com – meet, chat.

www.matchpurpose.com – chat, tours, meet.

www.datingforseniors.com – chat, meet, exchange..

www.seniormatch.com – dating, chat, meet

www.jadate.com – Jewish affiliated social site.

www.catholicmatch.com – Catholic affiliated social site.

www.christianmingle.com – Christian social site.

www.personals.yahoo.com – search "seniors".

www.match.com – dating/social.

www.eharmony.com - dating/social.

www.seniorfriendfinder.com – chat, social.

www.ymca.net – local community links to activities, social calendar, etc.

HOW SENIORS CAN FIND COMPANIONSHIP OR MARRIAGE

www.redhatsociety.com – the Red Hat Society for networking and support.

www.facebook.com – has senior pages by local area.

Churches – visit online or in person and search out social and activities calendar.

Activities - To meet active, interested and stimulating singles.

Your local senior center - usually features a variety of activities and opportunities!

Your local alumni association - many offer singles groups. Don't ignore your class reunions! Might ignite old flames!

www.exploritas.org – the Elder Hostel site for learning and travel.

Various cruise lines - frequently offer "55+" discounts on some of their ships and destinations. Search the specific cruise lines such as Azamara, Carnival, Celebrity, Cruised West for details.

www.cruisecritic.com – travel ideas – search "seniors".

Gallery openings – listed in local newspapers or newspaper websites.

Local library – posted local activities and groups.

Hobby and craft stores – may have group activities/instruction.

www.seniors.lovetoknow.com – lists group activities, but you must create a login.

Churches, church outings, socials - social opportunities, volunteer possibilities

Senior centers – investigate activities, game nights, bingo, etc.

Auctions –at auction houses, churches, schools.

Community senior newspapers – list activities.

www.ehow.com –search on "senior", how to join senior travel group, bus tours,

www.travelwithachallenge.com – active travel for older people.

www.50plusexpeditions.com – senior travel site.

www.SeniorTravel.About.com – travel for seniors.

www.frommers.com – search "senior travel".

www.smarterliving.com – travel site: try the 'senior' choice under SPE-CIALTY TRAVEL.

Volunteering – Being social while feeling good.

www.howstuffworks.com/ – different kinds of ideas and volunteer links

ncoa.org – National Council on Aging – volunteering through SCSEP (senior community service employment program) and CLIC (continuous learning and innovation community)

www.score.org – mentoring/volunteering as a retired business person.

www.seniorcorps.gov – excellent site that connects seniors with organizations

www.local humane society, animal shelter – volunteering with animals.

www.animalhumanesociety.org – pet care, volunteering

www.over50andoverseas.com – overseas volunteering.

www.local police and fire department – sponsor volunteer activities.

Your local university/college – volunteer opportunities and access to their alumni activities and social groups

Church volunteer programs – soup kitchen, daycare.

Goodwill, Salvation Army – have volunteer opportunities.

Community service volunteering – Neighborhood Watch, Welcome Wagon.

www.volunteersfortheblind.org – handicapped volunteering.

Schools – PTA – inquire about classroom reading, tutoring.

Churches, community centers – inquire about senior mentoring opportunities.

How Seniors Can Find Companionship or Marriage

Physical Fitness – For strong and healthy socializing.

www.seniorhealth.about.com/ -health information

www.fitness.com – search on "senior fitness"

www.nia.nih.gov – National Institute on Aging, guide to physical activity and exercise

www. nhtsa.gov – National Highway Traffic Safety Admin., search on "Stepping Out".

www.cdc.gov/physicalactivity/growingstronger/index – strength training.

www.aarp.org/walking – community walking program.

www.walkingtheworld.com – senior walking site.

www.seniorwalkingfitnessblog.com –senior walking and fitness site.

Mall walking programs – contact your local mall.

Churches – sponsor fitness, walking activities.

Community centers – sponsor exercise, fitness programs

Senior centers – sponsor exercise, fitness programs

City parks departments – sponsor walking, hiking group fitness activities.

Community senior newspapers – advertise exercise, fitness, activity classes and groups.

www.ymca.org – have senior fitness classes.

City governments – encourage biking and have listings of bike routes and groups.

www.fitness-singles.com – hiking and biking groups.

www.Seniorjournal.com/sports.htm – senior sports listings.

www.gorp.com – Great Outdoor Recreation Page – activity guide, adventure vacations, campgrounds.

www.seniorsoftball.org –International Senior Softball Association - softball activities, leagues – by states.

www.seniorsoftball.com – state specific also.

State Senior Games Association (google) – lists local senior activities.

National Adult Baseball Leagues (google)

www.usta.com -USTA Adult and Senior Tennis (google)

Volleyball tournaments – local community centers and parks departments list groups and tournaments.

The Arts - Meeting others in the worlds of culture and creativity.

www.artslynx.org – arts cross-referenced links.

Local art galleries – have openings, socials, lectures.

Local theater groups – senior discounts, ushering opportunities, acting classes or auditions.

College arts departments – in person or by computer listings of events, lectures, classes.

Google "seniors in the arts" – for ideas and opportunities.

Bookstore events – readings, book club postings.

Arts magazines calendars – i.e. Smithsonian magazine, New York magazine.

Public library – readings, volunteering, book club listings.

Community art walks – ask city hall, local galleries.

Museum free nights, reduced senior admission – inquire online or in person.

Museum sponsored events – tours, trips, special shows, openings.

www.communityarts.net – arts for seniors.

Senior Celebration of the Arts – in many cities – i.e. **pcacares.org -** Philadelphia Corp. for Aging

Enriching experiences in the arts – i.e. **wpas.org** – Washington Performing Arts Society

HOW SENIORS CAN FIND COMPANIONSHIP OR MARRIAGE

www.geezermusicclub.wordpress.com – Geezer Music Club senior social involvement with music.

Churches – choir programs, music events, music instruction

State and city Cultural Office of the Arts –activities and events.

Education and Learning Activities – Using your mind and socializing at the same time.

www.adulted.about.com – continuing education, classes.

www.adulteducation.org – many academic opportunities and ideas.

www.exploritas.org – programs for seniors at colleges.

Online courses – most colleges offer.

Extension courses – most colleges and universities offer.

Business Groups – a way of meeting other seniors that may lead to a good bottom line.

www.aarp.org – search "jobs for seniors".

www.entrepreneur.com/businessideas/789.html – career ideas for seniors.

Lions club, Rotary Club, Chamber of Commerce – opportunities for business networking, mentoring.

www.nytimes.com, other newspaper websites – search for "employment seniors".

www.jobster.com/find/people/about/elderly – networking opportunities for seniors.

Support for living – when you or someone you love needs extra care.

www.portal.hud.gov/– under TOPIC AREAS choose 'information for senior citizens'.

YOU DON'T HAVE TO LIVE ALONE

www.eldercarelink.com – caregiver referrals.

www.aarphealthcare.com - Medicare options

www.medicarerights.org – general questions about long term care.

Medicare Hotline – 800-333-4114 – immediate questions.

www.advancedseniorsolutions.com – general assistance.

www.caregiverhelper.com – questions and assistance.

www.seniorshelpersinc.com – companion ideas.

Marriott senior living services – private options

HOW SENIORS CAN FIND COMPANIONSHIP OR MARRIAGE

INDEX

You Don't Have to Live Alone